To James.

to commemorate

With our Love.

David and Shirley

HE HEALETH ALL THY DISEASES

"Bless the LORD, O my soul: and all that is within me, bless his holy name. Bless the LORD, O my soul, and forget not all his benefits: who forgiveth all thine iniquities; who healeth all thy diseases; who redeemeth thy life from destruction; who crowneth thee with lovingkindness and tender mercies; who satisfieth thy mouth with good things; so that thy youth is renewed like the eagle's."

Psalm 103:1-5

He Healeth
all thy
Diseases

EXHORTATIONS ON SPIRITUAL HEALTH
FOR THE DISCIPLE

Dennis Gillett

THE CHRISTADELPHIAN
404 SHAFTMOOR LANE
BIRMINGHAM B28 8SZ

1989

Chapters 1-18 first published under the title
Diseases of the Soul, 1975

This expanded edition, 1989

ISBN 0 85189 125 X

Typeset by Action Typesetting, Gloucester
Printed by Billing & Sons Limited, Worcester

FOREWORD

TODAY, for almost everyone, bodily health is a number one priority. When it fails, the enjoyment of life, with its hopes and ambitions, is hindered and halted. Vast amounts of money are spent every year upon getting well and keeping well. More and more, solemn warnings are being issued about the danger of eating wrong food, neglecting exercise and the harmfulness of drink and tobacco. Perhaps, as never before, health is a major issue in the nation's consciousness. People march to express their concern; they protest to demonstrate their fear; they jog to get fit and make the heart strong. It has become common for all kinds of people to do exploits for the purpose of raising money for medical research. There is abroad a real expectation that nowadays medical science will be able to find cures for diseases which at one time were regarded as incurable, and therefore death sentences. It is not unlikely that government could lose power over the nation's health and how well it is being serviced. Diseases, once quite unknown to the layman, are now the topics of ordinary conversation. Never before was good health regarded with such importance and pursued so assiduously.

For disciples of Christ spiritual health is even more vital. The Bible and their experience has taught them that just as the body fails and falters, so does the soul. There are some conditions which are true of both. After all, man is one whole, although he has different parts. The Apostle Paul speaks of "body, soul and spirit", but he did not teach that man existed wholly in any one part. The soul is that spiritual quality of human nature which makes man a rational creature, with conscience, emotion and will. The soul therefore is an inseparable part of man — it is the man himself. There are no souls without bodies, but the soul is the non-material element in the combination of parts which make the whole man.

In the realisation that spiritual sickness is a stubborn fact, it is enlightening to notice that many of its manifestations resemble diseases of the body. Or put the other way round, bodily sickness has its counterpart in soul sickness and occasionally the one is interlocked with the other. In any case there is a coalition of terminology which helps recognition of spiritual sickness in terms of the physical. In the pages which follow an attempt has been made to identify some of the diseases of the soul by the index of the bodily physician, but more especially to draw attention to the power of the Great Physician and his prescription for true health, revealed in the Word of God.

It is sent forth in the hope that it may be a provocation to any who read it to seek spiritual health with the same fervour and the same anxiety that energises the search for bodily soundness.

D. GILLETT

CONTENTS

1

DEPRESSION

THE very best people — especially the young — get depressed. The condition is often preceded by disappointment and frustration. New born zeal is full of optimism. The young see visions and dream dreams. The future seems full of promise and possibility. Life being what it is, the realisation falls short of the ideal. Limitation looms large as the experience deepens. The soul longs for the unreached — and is not satisfied. Disappointment invades the spirit. So much was planned — so little achieved. If only it had been better. So disappointment passes into discontent.

Discontent broods over the past and sighs doubtingly about the future. The vision is dislocated — men become monsters and walls reach up to heaven. Every way seems threatened with failure. The nerves are overwrought. Depression settles upon the spirit. The words of the Psalmist express the mood: "Who will shew us any good?" (4:6).

Sometimes people come to a depressed condition through weariness. Paul says, "Be not weary in well doing, for ye shall reap if ye faint not" (Galatians 6:9). Fainting is a sinking feeling — and sinking is another word for depression. Weariness is not tiredness; it is being dispirited, losing hope. Tired men can rest and soon be reinvigorated — weary men are sick. Every task begins with a sigh — every duty becomes a monotony. The sharp edge is blunted. The day is always dull — the earth always cold. The seed seems dead — the sower is weary. The spirit is at the mercy of the digestion and the weather. The face is pinched and the soul is shrivelled. The King's business is undone.

Self-interrogation is the first step to recovery: "Why art thou cast down, O my soul, and why art thou disquieted within me?"

1

(Psalm 43:5). Probe the fears and challenge the phantoms that haunt the spirit. At short range spectres are seen through. Fear enslaves — courage liberates. Venture with courage upon the naked word of God. Resist the temptation to relax. Remember that triumph comes by travail. Dull earth and apparently dead seed are the forces of harvest. Monotony is transmuted by faith. Reconstruct the golden vision of reaping. The husbandman needs patience as well as energy: ''Be ye also patient; establish your hearts'' (James 5:8).

God may be invisible but His ways are seen by the pure in heart. Fall back on God's promise of providential care, and rediscover that He careth for you. He quenches the parched soul and gives songs in the night. The weary may cast all their care upon Him. The Everlasting Arms reach lower than the lowest depression. Obedience is better than grief. Men are not saved by sorrow but by faith. When Elijah was over-wrought, God reassured him and sent him on a journey into changed surroundings. Let the depressed renew their trust in God, take a holiday and look to their general health.

2

HARDENING

THIS is not a disease of the young. They have their sicknesses, but this is rarely one. This comes with advancing years. As the bones get set, so sometimes does the spirit. The process is measured in years, not weeks. The symptoms are imperceptible at first. Often it takes a crisis to discover the condition. What has been inward for years suddenly becomes outward. In a situation which calls for soul sensitivity, hardness is discovered.

Hardening is recognised by a diminishing capacity to sorrow over iniquity. One day a man commits a dark, defiant sin. He is appalled and crestfallen. He can hardly believe it possible. The next time it happens he is shocked and upset, but not so much as the first time. The next time he does it reluctantly. The next time the reluctance is milder. At last he is not turning a hair. The writer of the letter to the Hebrews, by way of warning, has marked the process: ''hardened by the deceitfulness of sin'' (3:13). That which at first seemed like a silken thread, at last becomes an iron chain.

The deceit of sin is that it makes plausible that which ought to be repudiated and condemned. Slowly the conscience is dulled. The voice is silenced. The tears are dried up. The spirit is enslaved. Sin promises freedom and enwraps a man with bondage. Nearly always it begins with accepting a false argument — that is part of the deceit. So, if the process is unchecked, bit by bit a man becomes as hard as a nether millstone.

Another symptom is the loss of pity. The weak and the lame provoke no sympathy. The world's woes incite no tears. Those who weep are despised. Faithful words are met with an incredulous smile. Compassion for the ignorant is soon exhausted.

3

The Gospel is not proclaimed; the living water is left untapped. Thirsty souls are unrelieved. Hardening enables a man to be like this without a blush of shame, without a blanch of fear.

The peril is subtle. It may not have in it any sin which the world counts vulgar, but it leads at last to unbelief. Nearly always it begins ever so slightly with the first cooling of the passion for the Truth, the willingness to accept something lower than the highest, to settle for what is not the ideal. So a man who once was clear sighted is deceived. As the hardening process develops, the Bible gets dusty, fellowship is intermittent and private prayer ceases. To lose conscience and compassion is to lose two of God's greatest gifts. When the heart is hard, occasions for offence come easily.

Hardening is not incurable. Prevention is better than cure, but there is a remedy. Get to the open window and renew the lines of communication. God is found when He is sought in prayer. Distance is no object. It is possible to be overfed and undernourished if the food is wrong. Get the right food: "Man doth not live by bread alone, but by every word that cometh from the mouth of God" (Matthew 4:4).

The ecclesia is a home where souls are succoured in the hour of sickness. Under the influence of harmony and love, hardness gives way to humility, indifference to the joy of brotherhood. In spite of its imperfections, the ecclesia is the spring of strength, joy and compassion. There, with prayer and the ministry of the word, hardening may be healed.

3

HEART FAILURE

LUKE chapter 21 reveals that in the last days there will be an epidemic of heart failure: "Men's hearts failing them for fear." Then or now most spiritual heart failure is caused by fear — fear of deprivation; fear of the unknown; fear of the future.

Circumstances arise in which loyalty will result in loss. Faithfulness will mean forfeiting some material advantage. Some temporal advancement can be retained — only if principle is set aside. In contemplation of the disadvantage, courage is abated. Measuring the deprivation, the soul gets sick. The eternal things are held with light hands. Old convictions are dimmed by plausible arguments. The heart which ought to be garrisoned by trusting faith, falters and fails.

Fear of the unknown is fear of mystery, things in life which baffle the soul and fill it with foreboding: some suffering which makes no sense; some burden which is not deserved, but which cannot be shed; sowing love and reaping hate; a thorn in the flesh, which makes the heart sick. Why? When? Wherefore? The questions multiply and the mystery deepens. Life seems to be at variance with all that has been promised. Why does the Lord seem so remote? Is He after all an impassive God? Is omnipotence really righteous? In the face of the present mystery weakness turns to fainting and fainting to fear. The soul is disquieted, the heart is derelict.

Because the future is uncertain, it holds some fascination. There may be great things ahead, but who can be sure? With every possibility of success there is the haunting fear of weakness in the face of opposition. The best beginning may end worst. Yesterday's misfortunes may be repeated tomorrow. Past paralysis may strike

5

again. To the fretful soul the future is surcharged with failure. The neck is bent to disaster. Evil men and seducers wax worse and worse. The nations plunge into barbarism. The walls are broken down and the gates are burned with fire. The light gleams for a moment and then cruelty, crime and chaos sweep over the land. Hope is diminished — confidence passes into consternation. The soul is storm tossed and terror casts its shadow over a dreary landscape. ''Where is the promise of his coming?'' Men's hearts fail them for fear.

A failing heart may be mended, but being fortified against failure is better. Psalm 112 reveals the kind of man who is guarded against the assaults of fear: ''He shall not be afraid of evil tidings; his heart is fixed, trusting in the Lord'' (verse 7). The fixedness is rooted in faith. Stability is founded on breadth of understanding. A trusting heart knows it is better to suffer loss with the Lord than to advance without him. A man's life consisteth not in the abundance of the things he possesses. Status is a poor substitute for stature. To gain at the expense of principle is voluntary misfortune. To know how to abound and how to be in need, without fretfulness or folly, is to know the secret of tranquillity. When the spirit is detached from the transitory, the heart is fixed against the day of deprivation.

The trusting heart believes that nothing in the life of faith is outside the compass of the Lord's control. Underneath the deepest weakness are the everlasting arms. Sorrows are encircled and fears are cradled by the tenderness of the great God. In the very thing which seemed full of perplexity His love is discovered. His strength is made perfect in weakness. The purpose of God gets underneath rock bottom. By faith the perplexed heart may receive of His quietness and strength. Even hard things He will make to be the minister of good. The adversary proves to be a friend.

Evil tidings make the doubting heart hopeless. Religion seems to give its benediction to unbelief. Science bestows its powers upon the wrong people. But in the midst of darkness there ariseth light to the man of trusting faith. He knows the set time has come. The Lord is at hand. Because God has exalted him, nothing can dethrone him. No power on earth can defeat His purpose. The vision hath an end. He will arise and have mercy on Zion. Jerusalem will be made glorious. The wounds of humanity will be healed. All tears shall be

6

wiped away. Peace shall flow like a river. Sin will be finally vanquished. Death will be swallowed up in victory. In the assurance of things hoped for the heart is fixed, and the soul is fortified against the day of frightfulness. This man reads his morning paper with its evil tidings and then goes out to do his duty calmly and faithfully.

For this sickness the answer is plain. Get the heart fixed.

4

ULCERATION

THIS kind of disease means that there is a constant soreness in the soul. The disposition suffers from inflammation. There are places where the spirit is abnormally tender. Consequently the character is angular.

Rarely is anything right. Trifling things cause chafing. Those designed to please too often irritate. Ecclesial activities bring aggravation instead of joy. The opportunity to criticise is never missed. In innocent words some guilt is discovered. The innocuous is made to be injurious. The willing heart is labelled froward. Service is measured as self esteem. The fear of change becomes a phobia. Every new thought is suspect. The ecclesial temperature is always low. The meeting is cold. The Truth is going to the dogs.

Ulceration is rarely discovered by self diagnosis. A man's best friends can tell him, but too often the advice is regarded as an insult instead of a help. The treatment will not be self-administered; it will have to be applied by others. A man with a chip on his shoulder is a man with a burden. He needs succour, support and sympathy. Blunt shock treatment may occasionally succeed, but usually it does not. Men being what they are, the best treatment is the ministry of burning coals. Repaying angularity with things which are opposite. For hardness — gentleness. For suspicion — openness. For coldness — warmth. Nothing heals ulceration like a loving spirit. Kindness is a balm to the soul. Sympathy soothes the soreness.

People rarely complain about themselves. Nothing halts criticism like involvement. The worst thing for ulceration is the armchair. It is the place where thinking turns into brooding. Brooding breeds resentment. Resentment is like a child — it grows with nursing. Sometimes the effect of armchair resentment can be counted in round figures. Activity is good for soul and body. Give the critic a job.

The treatment must be specialised. Here is divine wisdom: "Consider one another to provoke unto love and good works." That means that every person is an individual. The thing which suits one is wrong for another. One man's succour may be another man's subversion. Healing ulceration is a matter of discernment. The things which provoke one person to love and good works may not be effective in another. The method must match the disposition of the individual. Jesus once said to his disciples, "I have many things to say unto you *but ye cannot bear them now.*" There may be a point at which a method of treatment becomes unbearable — for the time being. Therefore, use tact, sympathy and sanctified common sense. Take time — have patience. Rushing multiplies risking. Do not lose heart. You may have to settle for alleviation instead of cure. Soft water alters the shape of hard stones — but not overnight. New born people are still affected by old influences. "Consider one another . . ."

Ulceration usually has three levels — mild, chronic, acute. It is easily detectable in others — almost imperceptible in one's self. Anybody who has a suspicion about his soul's health, might do well to ask his friends.

5

AVAROMANIA

AVAROMANIA is an inordinate desire to get money and the things that money can buy. But the right diagnosis calls for precision. It is not getting money, but *loving* to get it. It is not possessing things, but possessing them *avariciously*. The infection is not measured by the amount but by the spirit. Sometimes poverty breeds the worst kind of covetousness. Sometimes people hold an abundance — with light hands. The disposition is the vital thing. Paul said, "The *love* of money is a root of all kinds of evil." John said, "*Love* not the world, neither the things which are in the world." Jesus said, "After all these *things* do the heathen *seek*." According to the King the supposed supremacy of things has its roots in paganism. That is why this disease is so serious. In the world it is fairly common — in the Truth it is rare.

It is easy to moralise about money when there is plenty — it is more difficult when the purse is empty. In the civilised world money is the passport to ease, comfort, and beauty. Gold is power. The world pays homage to those who have it in abundance, and reserves its admiration for those who make it consistently. But its limitations are evident. It can buy houses, food, soft beds, doctors and influence. It cannot buy homes, appetite, sleep, health and love. It can command the biggest and the most ostentatious. Think of the man in the parable — everything about him was big because of his love of wealth. Big barns, big house, big dinners — big funeral.

In the Bible covetousness is called idolatry. It puts something in the place of God, because it is reckoned more likely to bring success than trusting in Providence. It makes men blind to other men's needs, and fosters indifference to wrong doing. It breeds

10

complacency towards doubtful methods and complicity with dubious practices. Covetous men barter their principles and stifle their consciences, if the advantage can be measured in pounds and pence. Paul was right. It is a root of all kinds of evil. One of the root sins of humanity. In the letter to the Hebrews it is coupled with impurity.

The world loves things. It will do almost anything to gain them. Sweat, strive, lie and even die. Some people's idea of the world to come is a great abundance of things. To live for gaining things is to have lost the one thing worth having. Sometimes things are a hindrance to the man who seeks the highest and strives for the noblest. They become weights which have to be laid aside. Many a man loaded with things has found them a burden at last. Jesus said, "What doth it profit a man if he gain the world and lose his soul?" Life is more than having — it is being. The soul cannot be nurtured on things. Overfed with tinsel, it gets sick.

Fortunately the effect of this sickness on the soul is such that a man of God is driven to be rid of it. For those who have tasted the values of the Kingdom of God, a diet of husks cannot be endured for long. The flesh is fed, but the soul is emaciated. This disease brings discontent, envy and distrust — and so a stricken disciple turns back to peace, love and faith. "This is the victory which overcometh the world, even our faith." Faith will lay hold on these words: "I will in no wise fail thee, neither will I in any wise forsake thee." That promise is better than gold — more satisfying than things.

Plainly — the answer to being contaminated with this sickness is balance. The disciple needs money to provide things honest in the sight of all men. Things are not wrong in themselves — as long as they are servants and not masters. The Word of the Lord is the true guide: "Seek ye first the Kingdom of God and his righteousness and all these things shall be added unto you." When a man seeks first the virtues and values of the Kingdom of God, all other things are held in right perspective. The flesh is made subservient to spirit. The eye is opened — the ear is unstopped — the lost sense is restored. Life is God-governed. The demand to sweat and strain and toil for the transitory is seen to be folly. Use money and things but never, never imagine that they are more than *part* of human life. "Seek ye *first* the Kingdom of God . . ." In answer to the world's mania — this is the sublimest sanity.

6

BLINDNESS

SOME people believe that soul blindness is the deadliest disease of all. Jesus said that if it is not cured, it will lead to ditch death. Without doubt its consequences have sometimes been disastrous. Because of it men have opposed God's will and thought they did Him service. Those afflicted with it have called light darkness, good evil, and truth heresy. It enables people to be fastidiously careful to protect a tradition and carelessly indifferent about keeping a principle. In these circumstances how often have peripheral things been made central and incidental things made essential. The understanding becomes warped and religion emaciated. The place of peace and concord is turned into a battleground, where blind opinions war for supremacy.

In the day of our Lord some of the Pharisees were tragic examples of soul blindness. They believed in conformity to God's will, but their method made their objective impossible. Their conception of religion came to be wholly external and wrongly exclusive. For them righteousness was a complex system of religious habits. Life consisted of ceremonial purification, tithing of almost everything and fanatical hostility to the Gentiles. In pursuing this way of life, they developed their rules of conduct into absurdity. Gnats were strained out and camels were swallowed. The letter was emphasised to the point where the spirit was destroyed. The Sabbath was held to be sacred in a way which destroyed its holiest provision for the good of man.

The Pharisees held in supreme contempt all others they could not compel to their way of thinking. Said Jesus, "If ye had known what this meaneth, I desire mercy and not sacrifice, ye would not have condemned the guiltless"; or again, "Ye compass sea and

12

land to make one proselyte; and when he is become so, ye make him twofold more a son of hell than yourselves.'' Out of their ignorance of God's holiness and God's love, they were seeking to bring men to God and instead brought them to doom. The God they professed to extol they degraded. In the doing of it they became hard, critical, censorious. Self-exaltation made them to be hypocrites. The central nerve of the Truth was smothered. Religion was trivialised. Mark the estimation of the King upon this situation: ''Ye *blind Pharisee.*''

Blindness has several causes. Self-exaltation is one. Men who are interested in truth only in order to advance themselves never see it properly. The lap of the poor God fills with treasure, but the proud are sent empty away. Proud men may learn the words, but they rarely learn the lessons. ''To this man will I look, even to him that is poor, and of a contrite spirit, and trembleth at my word.'' Intellectual vanity is like a cataract on the eyes of the soul.

Another cause is the flesh mastered life. Jesus said, ''Blessed are the pure in heart, for they shall see God.'' Impurity hinders vision. Men see the spiritual in the measure in which they shed the sensual. Worldly preoccupation leads to double vision. The definition is poor and the perspective false.

Another cause is jaundiced prejudice, being so mastered by one aspect of truth as to throw the rest out of joint. Strong emphasis in a certain direction results in other things being neglected and the truth dislocated. That was the Pharisees' failure. They emphasised the external things to such a degree that the weighty matters of the law of life were almost obliterated. Prejudice is like a blank spot in the range of the eye. It permits sight only in certain directions. The rest cannot be seen.

Another cause is superficiality; a frivolous approach to holy things; an inability to see anything below the surface. Majestic things are not discerned by the silly. A mind fascinated by the spectacular is short-sighted. To be mildly curious is often to be self-blinded. Real vision calls for penetration. Superficiality is the myopia of the soul.

Recovery from blindness is possible. The first step is a recognition of the disease. So many blind people insist that they can see. This was the argument of Jesus in John's Gospel, chapter 9: ''If ye were blind, ye would have no sin; but now ye say, We see: your sin remaineth'' (R.V.).

The realisation of blindness may come suddenly with a shock, or it may come slowly by a gradual process of enlightenment. Once it has come, the curative forces are set in motion. A sincere man, realising his blindness, will at once be deeply aware of the value of vision. Impediments will be removed. Balance will be established. The word of God flashing light into dark places will purify the heart, and enlarge the eye of faith. With a new vision of the truth, cohesion and strength are multiplied. The earth is full of divine glory. A man humbles himself under the mighty hand of God. Whether it comes by earthquake or by gentle persuasion, there is no substitute for soul vision. Without it the people perish. Therefore get it at all cost — and fix your eyes on God and Zion.

7

DYSTROPHY

G IVEN thought, it speaks for itself. *Dys* — separation from; *trophy* — nutrition and growth. It means halted growth. We sometimes call it arrested development. To borrow an illustration: a condition of growth is good only if it occurs at the right time. At bud time the perfection of the bud is good and full of promise. If at blossom time the perfection of the bud remains, the promise has faded. At fruiting time the perfect bud means that the promise has failed. Three year old perfection in a child of three is excellent. The same three year old perfection at six is disturbing. At sixteen it would be disastrous. If nothing happens to recommence growth, the man will always be a child. He may wear a large overcoat and a bowler hat, but inwardly he is still in reins. The development which could have brought him to full manhood has been arrested. The muscles have grown but the mind has not.

This happens to the soul. The writer of the letter to the Hebrews in chapter 5 spoke to some who ought to have been teachers but were still pupils, living on milk instead of solid food; babes instead of full grown men, whose senses were unexercised and whose discernment was weak. At Corinth there were disciples whose spiritual anabolism* could not permit the taking of meat — to the dismay of the Apostle Paul (1 Corinthians 3).

Symptoms

Think of the symptoms. Sometimes an abnormal preoccupation

*Anabolism: "The process, in an organism or living cell, by which nutritive material is built up into living matter" (*Oxford Dictionary*).

15

with the fundamentals of the Truth which constantly asks for re-assurance about their certainty; an almost morbid interest in "difficulties" or the opinion of supposed experts on this question or that. Let not these sentences be misunderstood. The fundamentals are vital as a foundation upon which to build or as roots through which the tree draws its strength to grow. They ought never to be the source of doubt or disquiet. Constantly digging up trees to examine the root systems tends to hamper growth.

Another symptom is a naivety about the harmlessness of worldly forces, which to discerning men are spiritually dangerous. Another is the tendency to refer to the Truth as though in some way detached from it; to talk of being baptized into the movement, instead of into the fellowship of the redeemed; to speak of the ecclesia as "you" instead of "us"—with a readiness to shed responsibility for the corporate life of the meeting; a lack of desire to communicate to the unsaved the word of salvation; an unconcern about old habits and an unwillingness to burn old bridges.

Causes

Sometimes the symptoms reveal the causes. One cause of soul dystrophy is lack of conviction. Growth presupposes life and where faith is weak the life is atrophied. It is having the ethic without the dynamic. People in this condition tend to take their convictions second hand, believing something because someone else believes it. It never works. One man's grace is not sufficient for two. A man's conversion must be his own, else it will fail him at last. Mere consent is not the same as positive conviction.

Another cause is carnality; the fostering of some indulgence which ought to be repudiated. The cause of the Corinthian dystrophy was given by Paul in these words: "for ye are yet carnal." Sin condoned, excused, justified, paralyses the power to grow. In the letter to the Hebrews growing men were those who could discern the good and reject the evil. Poor health comes from wrong living— too often. The belly is filled with husks, but the spirit is starved.

Another cause is lack of love: love for the truth for the truth's sake; love for God's other children; love for ruined men in need of redemption. Paul says, "Love never faileth", and the verbs he uses are so revealing. Love beareth, believeth, hopeth and endureth. A

16

life lived within the compass of these forces is a life of growth—and where they are not is dystrophy.

Ponder the forces which can end dystrophy and restore development. This is not achieved by the human will, for no man by taking thought can add one cubit to his stature. Given life and health, growth is a divinely natural thing. It is not enlargement from without like a snowball rolling down a hill; it is enlargement from within, as an apple develops and matures on a tree. Paul says that the forces are available to promote growth: ''Unto each one of us was grace given ... that we ... speaking the truth in love, may grow up in all things into him, which is the head, even Christ'' (Ephesians 4:15,R.V.). Where the soul is yielded to these forces— the forces of grace—the growth will be into the likeness of Christ, an approximation to his character.

The forces of grace are the means of life. The means of life, whether for soul or body, are unmistakable: food, air and exercise — of the right kind and in the right proportions. Food is the Word of God — read, pondered and answered with regularity. Air is the right atmosphere in which to grow — namely that fellowship with God through Jesus Christ, which is achieved through prayer — a lifting of the mind and heart to the throne of the most High God through the High Priest of the Universe; in the secret place or in the market place — prayer as an habitual thing. Exercise is working for God's cause wherever it can be advanced; in the ecclesia, all the enterprises which teach His word, succour His children, hallow His Name; in the world, taking all the opportunities to proclaim His purpose, halt the spread of corruption and set His love on ruined men.

Although growth is not achieved by the exercise of human will, human responsibility is to co-operate with the forces of grace for the realisation of spiritual development. So the dystrophy may be ended and the new life revived and provoked, slowly at first, but surely at last.

The method is clear: discover the cause of the disease, recognise it and shed it; submit to healing forces of the Truth, and the scars will be obliterated. The lost years will be restored. The mildew will be halted. The promise of fruit will be realised.

17

8

PARALYSIS

IN a condition of normal bodily health moving the limbs is an act of will. It may not seem like it, but motion is a volitional thing. The mind has command of the muscles. Instantaneously one responds to the other.

Paralysis is a condition where there is a will to move, but the limbs do not respond. The mind has lost command of the muscles. The brain may insist, but the sinews refuse. The condition may be total or partial; the whole body or certain limbs only. Whichever way it is, in the affected area there is helplessness.

Soul paralysis is similar, but worse. The will has no authority. There is perception but no power. There is conception but no control. There is aspiration but no ability. "That which I would do, I do not." But it goes deeper. In this kind of paralysis not only does the spirit lack power, but the appetites control the will. The flesh dominates the spirit. "That which I hate, that I do." It is self rampant and self masterful; the soul subservient and the spirit imprisoned. Old habits are fostered and fed. Hands undo good work. Feet walk along the byways of evil. There is riot instead of restfulness, ease instead of effort. Right things are neglected, wrong things enterprised. There is no power to halt the forces of corruption. "What I do is not what I want to do, but what I detest" (N.E.B.). In the affected area there is helplessness. This is paralysis at its worst.

Apart from the endemic nature of some kinds of paralysis, its causes are more usually discovered in one particular thing or another, one supreme point of weakness, one outstanding difficulty; some lust of the flesh or some pride of life; some demoralising habit or some carnal desire; some force which has the effect of sapping the strength and paralysing the soul's energy. "One thing thou lackest" is spoken to every man who is made impotent by the withering forces of sin. "To whomsoever ye yield yourselves servants to obey, his servants ye are." It is a strange process. Some men consent to be slaves and tolerate the servitude. Others are mastered by forces which they detest, but from which they cannot escape.

Submitting to the Word of the Lord

Think of Mark chapter 3 and the man with the withered hand whom Jesus confronted in the synagogue. That man is the representative of all those who are disabled by paralysis. He stands for the palsied, the powerless and the prostrated. He was cured in the moment he submitted himself to the word of Christ. But there were things which preceded the submission. He needed to recognise his disability. He needed the conviction that the Man of Nazareth could be trusted, that he was not mocking his impotence, but leading him to a condition of healing. Then he heard the word of the Lord: "Stretch forth thy hand." If you can read the man's mind, in that moment he is saying, "That which I cannot do, I will" — and he did. He was brought face to face with the impossible thing — the heart of the disease. Through the word of Christ he defied the paralysis, exercised his will and found the power to move his withered limb.

It teaches us that when a man submits himself to the Word of the Lord he is linked with forces which are stronger and mightier than the power of spiritual disease and helplessness. It ought not to be surprising, for this is the essence of the Gospel. Fettered men can be set free. If it is not true, then we are of all men most pitiable. The man who once said, "That which I hate, that I do" is saying with humble confidence, "We are more than conquerors through him who loved us." So we may mark the process of healing. When a man recognises his disability and is prepared to venture his soul's health upon the promise of Christ, he is brought face to face with the master paralysis of his life. He is by the incisive word of the physician compelled to confess his secret habit; to bring out into the light the thing which fetters him and there to repudiate it. That which he could not do, he will begin to do. He is saying, "I cannot — but I will". Bit by bit there is ability in place of disability. Healing comes

19

in proportion to a man's submission to the word of Christ. Peter once in another context and for another reason said, "Lord, we have toiled all night and taken nothing, *but at thy word I will*". His submission was crowned with success. When human toil is ended and Christ is given the place of mastery, there is healing.

No Need to Despair

What of the man who says he wants to submit but cannot find the strength? He need not despair. There is grace to help in time of need. Ponder the word of Isaiah: "They shall mount up with wings as eagles, they shall run and not be weary, they shall walk and not faint." Fainting is revealed here as the opposite of walking. In this consideration men cease to walk through paralysis. Centrally, fainting and paralysis are so close as to be one. Fainting is to be weak, to lose strength, to feel the vigour passing, to realise the power is slipping away — at last to be helpless.

Hear the word of Christ: "Men ought always to pray and not to faint." Prayer is the opposite of paralysis. If fainting is paralysis, then prayer is power. It is mounting up with eagle wings, it is running without weariness, it is walking without feebleness. It is an attitude of submission, an act of co-operation. Through prayer the faltering heart finds strength to acknowledge the need and seek the submission which brings healing. Healing is not magic. It does not mean the end of failure, but it does mean freedom from that paralysis which makes failure inevitable.

Therefore, for the paralysed man who seeks to be healed, the word is clear: "Stretch forth thy hand."

9

DEAFNESS

B ROADLY speaking, there are three kinds of deafness. The first
is purely physical; some imperfection of the ear drum or
bone structure resulting in a failure to detect the audio vibrations.
As a result communication is hampered or ceases altogether. The
second kind of deafness is on a different level. There is no defect in
the mechanism of the ear, but the sounds which reach the ear do not
penetrate the mind. This is sometimes called mental deafness, because the mind is so preoccupied with one thing that it cannot
receive impressions about any other. One of the principal differ-
ences between physical deafness and mental deafness is that the first
is permanent and the second is intermittent. The third kind of deafness is observed in that condition where the sounds reach the ear and
are recorded by the brain and yet for some reason provoke no response in the soul.

This kind is the most serious, for because of it the mind is never
really illuminated, the heart is never stirred and the will is never
energised. The message of the Lord in the midst of the golden
candlesticks is a call to shed soul deafness: "He that hath an ear to
hear, let him hear." Associated with that hearing in an inseparable
relationship, as fruit is related to growth, is this word of exhortation:
"He that overcometh . . ." Whether it be the tree of life, the hidden
manna, power over the nations, the book of life, the new name, the
crown of life, the white stone, the throne of glory — the precur-
sor of all these is this: "He that overcometh." Always associated
with the master passion to overcome is the method of achievement:
"He that hath an ear, let him hear", as though to secure one is to
be assured of the other. It suggests that if a man is able to hear in
the way the King intends, then the victory is not in doubt. Mark,

therefore, how serious a disease soul deafness can be.

A Famine of Hearing

Amos leads us to the truth about deafness: ''Behold, the days come, saith the Lord God, that I will send a famine in the land, not a famine of bread, nor a thirst for water, but of hearing the words of the Lord: and they shall wander from sea to sea and from the north even to the east, they shall run to and fro to seek the word of the Lord and shall not find it. In that day shall the fair virgins and the young men faint for thirst'' (Amos 8:11 – 13). Notice the words carefully. Amos did not say that there was to be a famine of God speaking. It was not that God would refuse to communicate with His people, or had no more to say. It was not to be on God's part a capricious withholding of His word from those who desired to hear it. The famine came not from a failure in God, but from a defect in men. It was a famine of *hearing* the words of the Lord. It means that in the very presence of the word of God, spoken and continuously revealed, there was a condition in God's people which prevented them from discerning it. It was not that God ceased to speak, but that men lost the power to hear. It was soul deafness.

Notice the outcome: a great restlessness, resulting in utter failure. ''They shall wander from sea to sea and from the north even to the east . . . in that day shall the fair virgins and the young men faint for thirst.'' When those who are called to find rest in God try to seek it without Him, the bed proves too short and the covering too narrow. There is restlessness when those who once were in touch with the Infinite, lose the consciousness of its authority. Thereafter the music is lost, the exaltation is dulled, the sense of assurance is gone. Life becomes superficial and the deepest things are never realised. At last there is failure. Failure through famine is the worst of all. Notice how Amos describes it: ''In that day shall the fair virgins and the young men faint for thirst.'' He chooses the brightest and the strongest to illustrate and signify the awfulness of the failure. Those most able to endure are those who will faint. The highest powers, lacking true inspiration, will perish. All through being deaf to the words of the Lord.

Idolatry the Cause

To know the cause is to understand the cure. Amos reveals it: "They that sware by the sin of Samaria, and say, Thy god, O Dan, liveth; and, The manner of Beer-sheba liveth; even they shall fall and never rise again." The sin of Samaria was the worship of the calf. The worshippers swore by it and said, "Thy god, O Dan, liveth". Here is a great principle. If the true God is dethroned, ere long His voice is not heard. Deafness follows idolatry. When the creature is substituted for the Creator, the senses are hardened and the powers are weakened. Idols become a burden because they have to be carried. Isaiah said it: "Bel boweth down, Nebo stoopeth . . . they are a burden to the weary beast." Any man who is satisfied with something short of the Truth is on the way to famine. To come to terms with the ungodly is to prepare an idol. To magnify self and do homage is to make a graven image. These are the forces which seal men's ears to the Truth. If the god is insensate, so are the worshippers at last.

Mark the cure. When the idols are banished, the famine is over. Cleanse the temple and God reigns. Shed the impurity and the ear is unsealed. The Truth unveils her face not to the clever but to the humble. When the sin of Samaria is ended, the Word of God flashes and flames with new light. There is rest for the weary wanderer. The music is restored. The young virgins are pure. The young men are strong. The emasculated soul is healed. "He that hath an ear, let him hear."

10

AMNESIA

A MNESIA is loss of memory, resulting often in loss of identity. It comes through shock, or concussion or some interference with the circulatory system. Suddenly a man's recollection of the past is gone. He knows he is somebody but cannot remember who. His family are strangers. His home town is new territory. Familiar ways are unrecognised. Old friends become new faces. The associations of years are suddenly severed. Valuable antecedents are lost. The wisdom of past experience is dried up. The ties with life's lessons are cut. The memory of past joy is gone. The agony of yesterday's sadness is not recalled. The past tense has ceased — for good or ill.

A Comparison with Old Sadness

Suddenly becoming a new person is often good — but not in this way and for this reason. Often new endeavour is spurred on by a recollection of past failure. New joy is made more joyful by a comparison with old sadness. The memory of past deliverance gives hope for the future. To be able to remember is a blessed quality at all levels of living. How we live in the future is connected inseparably with how we have lived in the past. A realisation of the contrast will give perspective to the amended life. Remembrance of past victories may rekindle a fire in the soul. Some trial faced and mastered, then recalled, may give inspiration for facing the next with fortitude. Retracing the way thankfully tends to increase faith and rally the spirit. It is a blessed gift to be able to remember. Amnesia is a great handicap.

It has to be recognised that there are some things best forgotten. Sometimes memory lingers on the wrong things. Brooding on past

24

faults may imperil the future. Mourning over past folly may paralyse the will. Fretting over what might have been only aggravates the nerves. Gloom tortures the mind. Sometimes the wrong sort of remembrance only holds men captive. They are content to live on worn out experience — and the future is barren. A tenacious memory may bring despair. A man may be fortified by the past; but if he is a man of faith the real attraction will be in the future. The best is yet to be. A broad back to the past and a shining face towards tomorrow. In one place the Apostle Paul makes forgetfulness a condition of progress. There is a forgetfulness which is a thing of grace, but it is very different from Amnesia. One will lead to reaching the goal — the other to missing the mark.

The Apostle James has marked it for us. ''Be ye doers of the word, and not hearers only, deceiving your own selves. For if a man be a hearer of the word and not a doer, he is like a man beholding his natural face in a glass: for he beholdeth himself and goeth his way and *straightway forgetteth what manner of man he was*'' (James 1:23 – 24). This is amnesia of the soul. James is anxious to teach that hearing only leaves an impression which can be soon forgotten in certain circumstances.

Hearing and Acting

Hearing is good but the Truth is realised most by hearing made incarnate by obedience. Indeed a man who only hears and never acts is really half false. Everything we do — good or bad — tends to permanence. Every choice taken leads more in the direction of that choice. The man who hears and never does, has no permanent realisation of what he ought to be like. His choices such as they are lead him to nebulosity. Indolence and disobedience at last cloud his memory. The circulatory system of the soul is blocked. He forgets who he really is or ought to be. One day somebody who knows what he once was says, ''I am surprised to see you in this place — I thought you were a Christadelphian.'' Far away a bell is ringing, but the sound is uncertain and the call is unrecognised. Amnesia is a great handicap.

Jesus, in the parable of the two builders, warned us against the things which cause it. At first sight it might be said the rock in that story was the Word of God. Careful reading will tell us otherwise.

The man who built his house upon the rock was the man who heard the sayings of Christ *and did them*. The man who built on the sand was he who heard the same sayings and did them not. So in this parable the Word of God became rock for the man who obeyed. For the other the same Word of God sealed his doom. When he built his house it was really his tomb. In Peter's second epistle (1:5 and onwards) he lists all the blessed virtues which make for fruitfulness. If a man lacks these things, Peter gives us the reason — *"he hath forgotten that he was purged from his old sins"*. As Moses stood with the people of God in the plains of Moab before they entered the good land, he said, "And thou shalt *remember* all the way which the Lord thy God hath led thee these forty years in the wilderness ..." Centuries afterwards Ezekiel, in telling Israel the reason for their disastrous failure, speaks God's word and says, "Because thou hast *forgotten* the days of thy youth, when thou wast naked and bare ..."

Amnesia is a disease which needs to be taken seriously. It can lead to an eclipse of faith, and when faith is smothered the worst can happen. For the man who finds his soul-memory is bad, let him get back into the real fellowship of the ecclesia. Leave the perimeter — come into the centre. Let him shake off slackness and gird himself for the real business of the Truth. Present duty done lovingly will sharpen the memory and fill the soul with humble satisfaction. Forget the past and its lost opportunities — remember God's leading and His love. True identity will be established. Old friendships renewed. The memory of past joy recovered. The promise of true life rediscovered. On the distant horizon are signs of a new day. God never forgets those who remember His will and love to do it. When they are healed, they are healed to serve — now and hereafter.

11

GLOSSITIS

G LOSSITIS is inflammation of the tongue, resulting often in the organ becoming swollen and enlarged. In good health the tongue sits comfortably and neatly inside the lower jaw, actively fulfilling its function, but without obtrusion; instinctively doing its part in the formation of words, recording flavours, assisting mastication. With so much movement it is a marvel that it is not pinched between the teeth — but it rarely happens. There is, it seems, a built-in system of synchronisation whereby when the teeth meet, the tongue just escapes. When the tongue is inflamed and swollen it at once becomes obtrusive. Its true functions are hindered and movement becomes painful. Because of its enlarged condition words are malformed and sensitivity is dulled. Normal diet is restricted and things once appetising lose their flavour. The mouth tastes bad.

To the physician often the tongue is a barometer. Its appearance tells him of unseen abnormalities. It is an outward sign of an inward condition. Sometimes it gives insight into deeper and more serious failures. Its condition may signify that other parts of the body are not functioning effectually. It may tell that healthful harmony is disturbed.

The Tongue an Outlet

This diagnosis is even more true of the soul. According to the Apostle James the tongue is an unerring sign of spiritual condition. Like mercury the tongue tells the temperature. As the fever increases the tongue becomes expansive. Its output is very often the most telling projection of what a man really is. That is why by our words we shall be justified or condemned. That is why the unpremeditated activity of the tongue will have to be accounted for in the day of judgement. The absolute nature of the Apostle James' teaching about the tongue is often overlooked. He says it can *defile the whole body*. Jesus said that the forces which defile come from inside. The tongue is an outlet for internal influences, some of which are tainted with defilement. "The things which proceed out of the mouth come forth from the heart." In the list are evil thoughts, murder, false witness and fornication. At the worst stage of the disease the possibilities are awful. That is why James is so absolute.

The Apostle does not beat about the bush. He says emphatically, "The tongue is a fire." He means that by it the spirit is inflamed. "Behold how great a matter a little fire kindleth." In the R.V.: "Behold how much wood . . ." James' wood is a forest. A forest fire is a fearful thing — started sometimes by one careless ember, multiplied many times as it spreads: in James' metaphor — a wheel that catches fire as it goes. Think of it on a practical level. Sometimes those who meet together on Sunday and speak of love and fellowship, on Monday change their overcoat and say things which are harsh, unloving and censorious. As it spreads, the fellowship is fevered and friendships are soured. The ecclesia is harmed and the cause of the Truth is hindered. The smouldering fire runs on and the innocent are scorched and blistered.

The evil of slander

Think of it in another way. Very properly we are instant upon our defence of true doctrine. If words are spoken which question the faith, in the cause of truth the doubtful words are refuted and condemned. But it could be that the tongue which is pure in doctrine is heedless in the matter of another man's character. A cruel word is uttered carelessly. A doubtful insinuation is made irresponsibly. An emphatic silence is entered artfully. A shoulder is shrugged tellingly. The mischief is at work and a man's reputation is injured. If what is said is half true, then it is also half false. If it is half false it is wholly wrong. The Truth is indivisible — whether about doctrine or disposition. All our fidelity about the faith can be spoiled by our carelessness about calumny. Slander is so difficult to arrest once the wheel has started to turn. James says it is set on fire of hell. He means it is devilish. The first meaning of "devil" is slanderer. Too often the inflamed tongue magnifies evil and diminishes good. In the final stage it may result in assassination of some other soul.

James urges another point. The inflamed tongue is divinely unnatural. God created this organ so that men could bless and not curse. A fountain is faithful to its source. A tree is obedient to its own law. Both are divinely natural. A sweet fountain does not yield bitter water, neither does a vine bear figs. A tongue blessing God and cursing man is an awful contradiction. Every bubbling fountain and every fruitful tree protests against it. James says it plainly: "My brethren these things *ought not to be*." When it happens, it arises out of an unnatural and therefore diseased condition.

Co-operation

Soul glossitis is curable — else the human situation would be pitiable. No man by himself can tame the inflamed tongue. The solution is in the wisdom from above. The process of recovery may well begin with a realisation of how destructive the disease can be, how barren the landscape can become. As the desert teaches men to love water, so the stunted, graceless, unseasoned condition of the soul drives men to seek that which is wholesome and healthful. "The mouth of the righteous is a fountain of life" (Proverbs 10:11, R.S.V.). In the New Testament slander is coupled with idleness and James' solution is this: "Let him show by his good life his works in meekness of wisdom." So here is a good start — get working. Co-operate with those whom previously there has been a temptation to condemn. In the co-operation there is cleansing. In closer fellowship on a working level denunciation can give way to devotion. Antipathy is mastered by activity. Malice is ended by ministration. In working together men tend to share their common failings and are thereby equipped to recognise the common good.

Meekness of wisdom teaches us that we tend most easily to recognise in others the faults we are most familiar with in ourselves. It constrains us to urge in defence of our brother's weakness all the arguments we claim in defence of our own. It enforces the truth that those we do not like and those we suspect are also made in the image of God and, being in Christ, are in God's family. It provokes the exhortation not to assault with the tongue the man for whom Christ died. In this way recovery is surely advanced. Under this humbling discipline a man at last may come to recognise with joy the faithfulness of those he once impeached. It means that instead of deadly poison there is purity, and instead of restless evil there is peace. First pure, then peaceable. So with purified tongue man may bless God — and bless man, made in God's image.

Love

Because the inflamed tongue is a symptom of some impurity of the heart, in the end the best cure is love — ''out of a pure heart and a good conscience and faith unfeigned''. Paul says: ''Love vaunteth not itself . . . is not provoked, taketh not account of evil.'' It will have to be exercised first and most by those who have felt the sting of tongue fire. The truth reverently established. Discipline compassionately applied. Restoration lovingly made. Encouragement faithfully given. This is the blessed antiseptic for the fevered soul. By its therapeutic power all inflammation can be ended.

12

HYPOCHONDRIASIS

HYPOCHONDRIA is a condition in which a person enjoys bad health. He is morbidly satisfied to be, or seem to be, unwell, having a melancholy interest in disease, an unjustified preoccupation with illness. Every insignificant sign becomes a symptom of some terrible disorder. Little twinges, sighed about, soon become agony. The external is always the proof of something in the dark interior. A fatal defect is surmised and soon it is incurable. Sooner or later, the patient is half glad to join the army of the world's unfit. They squat at the gate and long for sympathy. They resent the suggestions that things are not so bad, half jealous of somebody who might be worse, willing to be treated but sure it will be fruitless. Crutches are better than confidence. Sometimes men are crippled by choice.

Faith Mixed with Pessimism

There are spiritual hypochondriacs. Sometimes they are revealed by an easy readiness to proclaim that all is lost. Someone will say, ''I know that I shall never be in the kingdom of God, but I am glad to help others to get there.'' As the condition advances, they find satisfaction in despair. Their chains are forged with unbreakable steel. By comparison other men's chains are made of silk. Faith is always mixed with pessimism. The old habits of slavery have to be nursed. It is sometimes justified by, ''I have always been like this — I cannot change.'' It suspects that the forces of heredity and environment are too strong for the Gospel. An echo of those upon whom the Apostle James remarks — those burdened by a fatalism which tended to blame God for the failure to master their passions: ''Let no man say when he is tempted, I am tempted of God . . . ''

31

Hypochondria fosters miscalculation. Too easily it concludes evil to be invincible. It makes friends with that which cannot be mastered. The best we can hope for is to minimise mischief — not destroy it. Failure is too strongly entrenched to be dislodged. There is talk of victory, but the forces of iniquity march unhindered. If they cannot be beaten, with reservations they will have to be joined. ''Let us eat, drink, and get what joy we can out of being miserable.'' To the despairing this appears sane and reasonable.

The people of God at Kadesh-Barnea exhibited symptoms of hypochondria. They had no confidence that their situation could be changed. They were cowed by walled cities and giants. The milk and honey hung in doubt — but they were sure of the leeks and garlic. They could not venture on the Word of God. Their faith was partial. God's description of it was this: ''They have not wholly followed me.'' Somehow they could not bring themselves to believe that success was possible. Deliverance from Egypt is one thing, but triumph in Canaan is another. They had escaped Pharaoh's penalty, but dare not lay hold on the new life in the good land. The master principle of possession is faith. They could not enter in because of unbelief. That is the sadness of this trouble. It leads men to nurse their failures, to cling to their infirmity, to be content with their disability, to be half pleased with their prejudices, to advertise their adversity, to sit tightly in their bath chairs and hold fast to their crutches. Thus the Truth for them becomes half false.

Set at Liberty

The Truth is not just an arrangement whereby men who ought to die, can escape. It is a superlative declaration that ruined men can be remade at the spiritual centre of their life — now and hereafter; not just deliverance from a penalty, but the revelation of Divine righteousness at the disposal of man; not just amelioration, but altogether renewal. Salvation is not only deliverance from death, not only forgiveness of sin; at last it is the power to do right, to master the antagonistic forces of heredity and environment. The enfeebled will is empowered. The paralysis is healed. The bound soul is set at liberty.

Those who suffer from this disease deserve help and encouragement. For them too often there are days of despair when the joy of life turns rancid. Too often there are dull days, when the lustre is lost and the shadows stretch ahead. There are days of doubt when Egypt seems nearer than Canaan, when to nurse the failure is easier than striving for the victory. The cure is through confidence. Recovery comes through a restoration of trust. The afflicted must be helped to the conviction that their condition is not unique. They are not too bad for the Physician. They will be no good without him. He believed that broken men were worth dying for, in spite of their bad health. He knew the very worst about men, but clung tenaciously to the belief that in them he could realise the best. To one who cursed and swore and denied he once said, ''When thou art converted, strengthen thy brethren.'' He knew that saints are made of sinners, willing to be remade.

The Response

But to his confidence there must be *confidence responding*. It is not enough to cry in agony. It is not enough to weep over sin. A man must resist the devil and trust unswervingly in the Lord. If the process does not work, then the fault is in the patient, not in the cure. If the fault is in the cure, then suffering and despairing men have been woefully deceived, for it is written, ''The gospel is the power of God unto salvation, *to everyone that believeth*''.* The important thing is not to procrastinate. This disease gets worse with neglect. Despair moves forward on a descending path. It may be difficult, but given time any difficult job becomes impossible. Grasp the means of grace which God has provided. Take the next step in obedience. Realise the power of the Gospel, not as a theory nor only as a doctrine, but in the experience of life, triumphing and ascending.

*As Paul puts it in Romans 1:17, ''by faith unto faith,'' the Lord's faith in his own provoking their faith in him.

33

13

HYPOTHERMIA

HYPOTHERMIA is low body heat and it could be argued that it is more of a condition than a disease. It is true that occasionally low body heat is medically induced in order to carry out heart surgery; in such cases it is controlled and therefore usually without danger. When it arises from other causes and is uncontrolled, people become ill and may sometimes die. So whether this kind of hypothermia is called a condition or a disease — the results can be very serious. The causes are under nutrition; living regularly in a cold atmosphere without sufficient bed coverings and personal clothing; lack of exercise.

In good health the normal body temperature is 98.4°F. The average clinical thermometer does not register temperatures below 95°F and hypothermia becomes serious at 90°F and under. At this stage the symptoms are a slow pulse rate, low blood pressure, the complexion is pale and may even be cyanosed. As the condition worsens the patient becomes more and more lethargic. There is almost total apathy towards those things which before were conspicuously of interest. The alleviation of hunger, pain or discomfort provokes no response. As the temperature falls the consciousness is disturbed. The mental reflexes are dulled and at last become comatose. If there is no help available, the coma moves into that level of unconsciousness from which there is no awakening. Hypothermia rarely troubles the young because normally they are well fed, mobile, active, have a sound circulatory system and hardly ever meet those circumstances which make for low body heat.

Love waxed cold

The spiritual counterpart of this condition is real enough and should be regarded very seriously. Jesus said it would be a peculiar feature of the latter days — ''Because iniquity shall abound *the love of many shall wax cold.*'' Soul hypothermia does not happen overnight — it begins slightly with the first cooling of the passion, the first lingering doubt about the triumph of Christ in his kingdom; the first nagging fear that sin may be invincible; the first willingness to let the secular displace the sacred; the first satisfaction with the second best; the first careless indifference to another man's need.

Very often the Bible Class is first to suffer from incipient hypothermia. Members may be absent for diverse and genuine reasons, but sometimes it is because that warm relish for the Word of God has cooled. Sooner or later those so affected lightly and regularly miss the appointed hour for the study of the Bible, and the joy of fellowship around its pages — *without being troubled.* As the passion weakens, so the soul loses its sensitivity. As the temperature drops, so the heart is dried up. Warmth tends to growth — heat makes energy. Cold leads to lethargy. ''The sluggard will not plough by reason of the cold; therefore he shall beg in harvest and have nothing.'' The arms once strong and resolute become weak and unstable. Thorns come up instead of roses. The face is a mask and pious phrases a cloak. Inwardly the spirit is chilled. Love is waxing cold — love of God, love of His word, love of His children.

Soul hypothermia is one of the opposing forces of healthy ecclesial life. It entices members on to the perimeter and the central things of the meeting are by-passed. Special efforts cease to be special and the effort is dilatory. Those who once went hot foot to the defence of the Truth too easily get cold feet. Burning zeal becomes smouldering ember. The river of life seems more like a glacier. Ardour gives way to apathy; fervour to frigidity. Even the prayers are cool, decorous and formal, and the business is done in cold blood. The springs of grace become frozen and the spirit of sympathy is benumbed. Other men's woes provoke little response and spiritual reflexes are palsied. The marrow is chilled; the soul is like marble — twelve months of winter each year.

Lukewarmness

The Lord hates hypothermia. Some of his strongest words were spoken against it: ''I would that ye were cold or hot; so then because thou art lukewarm and neither cold nor hot, I will spue thee out of my mouth'' (Revelation 3:15 – 16). Cold and hot, in this context, describe conditions which are honest and clearly identifiable, with no attempt at guile — that is why the Lord gives them preference. The Laodicean condition was a mask, a pretence, a sham. They claimed to be in good health, spiritually rich and replete in every sense, lacking nothing. It was all a parody. The health was sickness; the riches were burnt out ashes; the passion had flickered away. They were lukewarm and getting colder — the victims of hypothermia. One of the saddest things about this condition is that sometimes its causes are circumstantial. Warm men get cold by being in a cold atmosphere. With poor nutrition and no real spiritual exercise too easily a disciple becomes shrunken and forlorn, a prey to infrigidation.

The causes mark the remedy. One of the profoundest things the Bible says about its author is that God is fire. The dictionary says that fire is the evolution of light and heat by combustion. God is light — illumination. God is love — heat, passion. Combine the two and there is fire — sometimes consuming, sometimes warming and purifying. The remedy therefore is to get close to God and be warmed. Draw near to Him and He will draw near to you. Be nourished by His Word; be exercised in godliness. Shed the self-made narrow bed coverings which give no real protection and against which Isaiah utters a solemn warning in chapter 28. Seek to recapture the first love. Throw back the frontiers of frigidity and be clothed with humility. God resisteth the proud and giveth grace to the humble. Grace is like a warm spring flowing out over all the life of man. As the temperature rises, the old fire is rekindled; the embers are fanned into flame and the heart burns again; the pulse rate increases and energy returns. Across the barren landscape spring is come and the sound of the turtle dove is heard in the land.

14

OBESITY

OBESITY is sometimes another word for bigness, but not all bigness is obesity. Corpulence is comparative. Some people are naturally big and others get big unnaturally. Put another way — weight is not the problem; the danger comes from *over-weight*. Bulk hinders briskness. The proof is to see the writer on the parallel bars. Heaviness is a downward force. It imposes restrictions which can be frustrating and disappointing. Because of overweight that which we would do we do not. Sometimes it puts a strain on the heart which, if neglected, can be dangerous. Usually the best way of relieving the condition is to watch the diet and to take the right kind of exercise. It keeps the sinews in trim and the reflexes lively. Indolence leads to flabbiness. Turning the garden over in the mind does nothng for the muscles. Litheness and lethargy rarely go together.

All this is true of the soul. The man in the parable who died suddenly, probably suffered from heart trouble — but his soul was overweight. "Soul, thou hast much goods laid up; rest and take thine ease." Accumulating and resting and easing are enlarging forces, a surfeit of all those things which make men self satisfied and at last self mastered. So the soul is at ease when it should be disturbed, and content when it should be concerned, insensitive and indifferent to the things which are at the centre of spiritual life. So a man is held back, hindered and at last halted by soul obesity.

The writer of the Epistle to the Hebrews understood it: "Let us lay aside *every weight* and the sin which doth closely cling to us ..." (R.V. margin). The weight may be something attached externally which is perhaps easily shed. It can also be something developed

37

internally by the wrong kind of growth which is hard to lose. The word translated weight here is used to describe the swelling of the flesh, so it could refer to growth from within more than attachment from without. Men who mean business about the race do not run in overcoats, nor do they carry suitcases. If they are well trained they will not be burdened with that kind of flesh which ruins their performance.

Soul obesity brings a disinclination to be present when the Lord is remembered or His word proclaimed and pondered. The contemplation of ecclesial activity is accompanied by sighing instead of singing. Rest is more attractive than recreation. Theory appeals more than practice; thinking more than doing. Life mastered by surplus flesh is life nearsighted; life degenerating because of a dimmed vision of the ultimate, without real capacity to look unto Jesus the author and file leader of our faith.

Too often it is saying: ''What shall we eat and what shall we drink and wherewithal shall we be clothed?'' At last the only reality which matters is today and the dust. There is no communication with the invisible; no upward look; no sense of the spiritual; instead there is submission to the transient and the sensual, provoking a burning desire that has no satisfaction. At last the soul is weary, crushed by its own weight, fat with wrong feeding, locked by lethargy; descending is easy.

Spiritual Food — and Exercise

The way to recovery is evident. Feed rightly and get on the move. Two passages mark it for us: ''My flesh is meat indeed and my blood is drink indeed. He that eateth my flesh and drinketh my blood abideth in me and I in him'' (John 6:55 – 56). Devoted assimilation of the word and spirit of Jesus cleanses the consciousness, masters the flesh and energises the spirit. Once fleshbound and dominated by the nonsense of fleeting time, now liberated and under the discipline of purity and grace — horizoned by the forces of eternity.

The other: ''Exercise thyself unto godliness . . . for godliness is profitable for all things, having the promise of the life which now is and of that which is to come'' (1 Timothy 4:8). The word translated exercise is *gymnasia*, and from it a whole association of ideas come to mind. At this level a man who seeks success must be dedicated. The

38

spasmodic, half-hearted and casual make little progress. Underlying the words are the ideas of persistence, discipline and self-control. By contrast the things outlawed are intemperance, sloth and carelessness. Part of godliness is meditation, but thinking about it alone will shed no surplus weight, any more than it will add one cubit to the stature. The only muscles that get developed through talking are the muscles of the throat. Active fidelity to the principles of spiritual health are the only things which make for sanctified soundness. Sustained activity in the Lord's business, effort and resources placed at his disposal gladly and trustingly, constitute that exercise which develops godlikeness — because in the world of God things which have a common purpose take on a common likeness.

The flesh dominated life ladens the soul with weight and the clamant cry of its deepest aspirations is stifled and lost. The possibilities of the spiritual nature are never realised. A man's personality is buried in the dungeon of a prison built by his own folly. The Liberator has spoken these profound words: ''Come unto me, all ye that labour and are heavy laden, and I will give you rest. Take my yoke upon you and learn of me, for I am meek and lowly in heart; *and ye shall find rest for your souls.*'' This is the rest which ensures health. To such as are burdened and incarcerated, this is the release and the double cure. By this process the flesh will be made to serve instead of being served. The weight is lifted.

15

AGORAPHOBIA

THE Greek word *agora* means assembly or market place and therefore Agoraphobia describes a morbid antipathy towards public places. The condition is manifested by a fear of coming into the open. Safety is secured only by retreat into some inner place, away from other persons and apart from public activity. The possibility of having to face groups of people who may show interest or curiosity fills the mind with unusual anxiety. The contemplation of cultivating personal relationships generates alarm. External forces appear hostile: fellowship creates intrusion. Anonymity becomes a defence; isolation a bulwark. The sufferer, glad to be away from society, takes refuge in a self imposed imprisonment.

Care needs to be exercised in identifying the spiritual counterpart. It would be quite wrong to say that every shy soul or those reluctant to engage in outdoor preaching and canvassing are suffering from spiritual agoraphobia. Some people are naturally timid and some naturally pugnacious. Such attitudes arise usually from physical and mental causes, but soul agoraphobia is different — almost always it arises from moral causes; a reluctance to come out into the open as a disciple, because to do so would expose to some material disadvantage or loss of reputation; a tendency to seek refuge against identification by avoiding those occasions where affiliation with the people of God is obvious; a retreat into silence when to speak faithfully would reveal the fact that the speaker is a Christadelphian; a fear of being identified because discovery would uncover hypocrisy. So there is a strong tendency to hide away and a strong temptation to wear a spiritual disguise, to move incognito among other men. Religion becomes a secret and faith is furtive. Isolation becomes an opportunity to shed restraint. Every excuse is advanced to justify absence when the call is to come out into the open for Christ. The sufferer is glad to be in when others are out — and glad to be out when others seek to come in. The market place is the place of exposure and the secret closet a refuge — not for prayer but merely for protection.

Being a Companion of Christ

Jesus strongly reproved this condition both with his life and his words. The writer of the Letter to the Hebrews says of the Redeemer, "He endured the cross *despising the shame* ..." At the end of Mark 8 these words are recorded: "For whosoever shall be ashamed of me and of my words in this adulterous and sinful generation, the Son of man also shall be ashamed of him when he cometh in the glory of his Father with the holy angels." Says Paul in Romans 1:16: "For I am not ashamed of the gospel; for it is the power of God unto salvation to every one that believeth." To Timothy: "Be not ashamed therefore of the testimony of our Lord nor of me his prisoner ..." (2 Timothy 2:8). Peter in his first letter: "If any man suffer as a Christian let him not be ashamed ..." It is clearly the teaching of the New Testament that it is better to be a companion of Christ, even though it may bring a reduction in material gain and loss of worldly reputation, than to advance in both *but be without him*. According to our Lord to be without him for this reason is to be without him for ever. The call is to be with him in the light and in the open, in the market place as well as in the secret closet, in the ungodliness of a secular society as well as in the holiness of the sanctuary.

It has to be recognised that some of the symptoms are manifested by all of us occasionally, but that is not a disease. It is a disease when the condition becomes persistent and wilful, when there is a calculated assessment that public detachment from the Truth will protect human status and preserve worldly possessions. The cause of this condition is usually diminished faith and lack of vision. Those afflicted have lost trust in the promises of God and have become nearsighted. For such the horizon is misty and uncertain, the breaking dawn is clouded, the City of God is only half-real. There is a lack of respect for the recompence of the reward and a loss of power to account the reproach of Christ greater riches than the treasures of Egypt. Endurance surrenders as the invisible vanishes, while at the root of it all is a measure of unbelief.

Restoring Faith

Plainly the deliverance from this condition is by a restoration of faith. Sighing and brooding in isolation will do no good. The first vital step must be to venture into the open for Christ's sake. Be it ever so difficult, it has to be done — to break out of the prison of fear and frustration. Do it with others who trust, because in this condition faith can be contagious. Take your stand bravely for the Truth without shame. Leave the inverted life and find the true balance. Rediscover the harmony of right values. Know for sure that life on the plane of the material provokes a burning thirst and a devouring hunger which can never be truly satisfied. It is infinitely better to bear the reproach of Christ than to enjoy the pleasures of sin for a season — because, measured truly, the season is tragically short.

So venture forth upon the promise of God — "For himself hath said, I will in no wise fail thee, neither will I in any wise forsake thee, so that with good courage we may say, The Lord is my helper; I will not fear what man shall do unto me", reinforced in Hebrews 13 in the context of detachment from the love of money and an exhortation to be content with God's provision. The call is this — "Let us therefore go forth unto him *outside* the camp, bearing his reproach . . ." Those who come to trust that promise unreservedly will overcome soul agoraphobia and will go out openly with singing hearts and lilting steps and shining faces — for Christ's sake. *Their* eyes are open to the invisible and ears attuned to the eternal and they themselves enwrapped against the gaud and glitter of the world by the hope of those glorious things soon to burst forth in all the earth.

16

LAMENESS

L AMENESS speaks for itself but the causes vary and are not so evident as the effects. Sometimes people are born lame, like the man at the Beautiful Gate; sometimes they become lame through an accident, like Mephibosheth the son of Jonathan; sometimes they get lame through a rheumatoid or arthritic condition, possibly like the cripple at Bethesda. Whatever the causes, the sufferer is disabled and his mobility is impaired. Some malformation of the bone structure in the feet or legs, often with locking and swelling of the joints, makes movement arduous and balance unstable. To run is unthinkable; to walk is difficult; to climb is to attempt the impossible.

There are other conditions arising from other causes. Sometimes the spring of the sole becomes weak and the affected person develops what is known as flat foot. The springiness goes out of the step and walking becomes shuffling. The foot muscles become weak and as a result the toes droop. In this condition people have been known to stamp hard with the heel in an attempt to secure a better hold and a stronger thrust forward. Sometimes sensations in the lower limbs become blunted and as a result the movement of the legs is uncertain — the sufferer easily falls over. In another condition arising from wasted muscles, the steps become jerky and spasmodic, resulting in the affected one tripping easily over small objects. The legs once bent at the knees are painful to get straight and the limbs become rigid and unyielding. Control is enfeebled and muscle power devitalized. Lameness means impotence in one form or another.

That there is such a thing as spiritual lameness ought not to be in doubt. One certain proof is in Hebrews 12:12 – 13: "Wherefore

43

lift up the hands that hang down and the palsied knees and make straight paths for your feet, that that which is lame be not turned out of the way, but rather healed'' (R.V.). One of the sure evidences of lameness is uncertainty, a condition which brings hesitation and anxiety. Taking a firm step for the Truth is viewed with apprehension. It is better to sit quietly than to stand apart. Choices unmade are better than choices avowed. Going in circles seems safer than going straight. Somehow security is sought in convictions unformed and decisions unmade. Halting spirits too often halt between two opinions. Because of lameness you can never be sure where they stand. Willing to discuss, but never to decide; ready to moralise, but never to surrender; glad to argue, but never to commit themselves. The prospect of venturing trustfully causes the heart to flutter and the spirit to waver. Somehow the signs are always blurred and the line of cleavage too often undefined.

Fear the Root

Very often at the root of soul lameness there is fear. It is significant that in the passage from the letter to the Hebrews already quoted and which is cited from Isaiah 35:3, the prophet goes on, ''Say to them that are of a fearful heart, Be strong and fear not; behold your God will come with vengeance, even God with a recompence; he will come and save you.'' Too little faith and too much fear make the feet flat and take the lilt from a man's step. Forces which ought to make the soul spring with delight instead are drooping and descending. The man on the mountain had beautiful feet; strong for climbing and swift for service. The nature of the message he bore doubtless gave buoyancy to his step and garrisoned his heart against vacillation and retreat. Feet are not the most comely of our members, but they sometimes gain comeliness by swift running and glad going in the King's cause. When Enoch walked with God he became the forerunner of those who shed their fears and made straight paths for their feet and consequently mastered their lameness. Sometimes fear is like a ball and chain. Feebleness comes most to the unsure.

Sometimes those who suffer from lameness trip easily over small things. They are consumed by the incidental and are quickly rebuffed by the trivial; unbending about a rule but too often uncaring about a principle. As the gnats multiply, the camels slip by unrecognised. Again the soul tends to become insensitive when the powers are wasting. It is possible to shuffle in hob nail boots and other people's dreams can be trampled on even with flat feet.

Lameness is a sad condition — no man is a cripple by choice. It lacks exuberance and makes for pessimism. It neutralises other things which may be sound and good. There are those who long to leap, but their ankle bones will not respond. They settle for a squatting position, and too often they are regarded as a standing problem. They need the good news afresh from the man with beautiful feet.

Choose the Right Path

Lameness can be cured. The Hebrew writer said it: "Make straight paths for your feet, that that which is lame be not put out of joint *but rather be healed.*" It means that if the lame are going to attempt to walk confidently, they must choose the path carefully. Proverbs 4:26 says, "Make level the path of thy feet, and let all thy ways be established." If the first is ensured, the second will follow. Give up the ways which are uncertain, twisted and strewn with pitfalls. The healing comes first of all by an act of the sufferer's own will: "make straight paths for your feet . . ."

Secondly, the steps must be made trustingly and firmly — ready to venture on the Word of God, without demur. James says a double minded man is *unstable.* Instability is one of the symptoms of lameness. From Genesis to Malachi, from Matthew to Revelation — everything enforces the lesson that if man is to make any progress towards final and ultimate salvation he *must venture trustingly upon God's word.* Fear vanishes when faith revives.

Thirdly, accept gladly the hand of some other soul. At the Beautiful Gate of the Temple it was Peter's grip which put new heart into the lame man. There is a sense in which the crippled and the strong must get to close grips if any good is to be done. Let the strong be ready with practical help as well as good advice. Let the lame realise that sooner or later cotton wool and crutches have to be shed in favour of confidence and courage, so that, having found his feet, he too may carry with lilting step and a leaping heart the message of sympathy and salvation to such as are burdened and crippled and who squat at the Temple gate.

45

17

PYREXIA

THIS is not a disease in itself but a condition which accompanies certain diseases — especially those where a fever is induced. Pyrexia, therefore, is an abnormal rise in body temperature. Anything above 99°F is usually regarded as pyrexial and above 105°F is hyperpyrexial and serious. There are three types of this condition — continuous when the temperature remains above normal throughout 24 hours with only a slight variation; remittent when the temperature is above normal but shows a greater daily swing than in the continuous type; intermittent when the temperature passes from normal to a very high level in a short time and then returns to near normal again. With a rapid rise in temperature the patient may feel cold, whilst the skin is hot and dry.

Pyrexia is regarded as one of the body's defence mechanisms against invading organisms. It is caused usually by infection of some kind or some disorder of the nervous system which affects the heat regulating centre. Occasionally the injection of a vaccine will cause the body to overheat abnormally.

The Power of Heat

The soul can become fevered as well as the body. Heat is a powerful force, but its effects vary according to its location. In the greenhouse it advances growth rapidly — in the coffin it accelerates corruption. Heat is passion and when it warms the heart it can be a blessing; when it settles in the head or under the collar, it can be a curse. Cerebral pyrexia often inflames the spirit and scorches the reason. Collar heat makes men hasty in judgement and precipitate in action. By it a little fault is converted into a great wrong. As the temperature rises the back gets up. Heat makes the blood boil; inflammation makes the head sore; calefaction leads to choler, and as a result the spirits of others are wounded; feelings are hurt and friendship is soured.

Sometimes soul pyrexia is a defence mechanism against the invasion of light into dark places. A hot temper seeks to repel those forces which expose and unmask. More than once a soul desiring to advise and warn has been driven away by a fiery temper and a tart tongue.

Too often as the head gets hot the heart gets cold. The breast nurses feelings which encourage resentment and contention; so the spirit is testy, touchy and tendentious. That which began in hot defiance ends in cold isolation. That which started in high dudgeon ends in low despair. The sad thing is that this condition tends to separate the sufferer from the very forces which could alleviate his disability. Others cease to seek his company or ask for his help; invitations to co-operate diminish for fear of being rebuffed; discussion is avoided lest it should develop into hot disputation. Friends become cautious and acquaintances become indifferent. Men who ought to be open and artless become furtive and shuffling. Fellowship in the ecclesia is fevered and oppressed by pyrexia.

Temper Trouble

Almost everybody at some time has temper trouble. An occasional outburst of anger is understandable — may even be justified. This is not pyrexia. It is interesting to notice in the Bible men *occasionally* fail in the very thing for which they are notably strong. Abraham, the outstanding example of faith in the Old Testament, once adopts a subterfuge about Sarah out of fear for his own safety. John Zebedee, the apostle of love, is calling down fire upon the Samaritans, because he had been rebuffed. Peter, the man of rock, is craven when he is challenged by a servant girl. Moses, the meekest of men, once loses his temper. This is not pyrexia. The diagnosis is concerned with that condition where the loss of control over passion is regular and conspicuous. In some people it is continuous — they are always out of humour. With others it is remittent or intermittent — from being normal, suddenly they are fractious, peppery, choleric. Perhaps the two outstanding examples of this condition in the Bible are Cain, who in a state of hot vicious temper slew his brother, and Saul who out of a condition of hot impatience usurped the power of the priesthood.

The Power of Love

One passage in the New Testament marks the answer to pyrexia — 1 Corinthians 13: ''Love suffereth long and is kind; love envieth not; love vaunteth not itself, is not puffed up . . . is not provoked.'' This proclaims that *love is long tempered*. One of the fruits of the Spirit is long-suffering — the habit of love. Another is temperance, which means self control and is the opposite of hot temper. Self control is the victory of love. The answer therefore is a sincere and serious attempt to seek and apply all the means of grace whereby the face and force of love can be expanded and developed in the soul. The Gospel reveals that Christ is set upon winning his victory in each individual heart, so that step by step a man's life becomes love-mastered and love-driven. Pyrexia is a difficult condition, but not too difficult for the one whose strength is made perfect in weakness. In submission to him the fevered soul is healed.

18

EUPHORIA

EUPHORIA is an unjustified optimism about the inevitability of good health. It is an unbalanced condition, blind to the dangers and indifferent to the forces which cause disease. It scoffs at that prudence which sane men exercise in defence of their health. It mocks those rules which are calculated to avoid sickness. Sensible precautions are regarded as fads and fancies. Its favourite sentence is, "There is nothing wrong with me." There is talk of people who live to be 90 and break all the rules. Worrying about health is said to be more likely to cause disease than cure it. The future is always bright, conditions are always fortuitous. Safeguards are silly. Sometimes and too often at the age of say 48, after a heavy meal and hearty game of tennis, this man, mastered by Euphoria, drops dead.

Ponder the spiritual counterpart. It is an unjustified optimism about the inevitability of spiritual success. Unjustified because it continually violates the conditions which make success possible. It wants to hear nothing of prudence, vigilance and watchfulness. Those who warn of worldly dangers are said to suffer from spiritual belly ache. It is blind to the effects of those forces which balanced men view with respect and awe. It flirts with temptation in the conviction that the devil has been over rated and the chances of victory under sold. It sees no danger; senses no deprivation; is hardened to failure by synthetic confidence.

The channels of strength upon which other men depend are neglected and almost despised. It is indifferent to other men's experience without a tremor. Talks glibly of the Kingdom of God and will not understand that rebels are excluded. Takes refuge in the love of God and will not be awed by His severity. Believes the livery of discipleship is protection against judgement. Euphoria is not assurance based on faith provoked by reverence for the promises of God. Euphoria is false confidence engendered by a misunderstanding of God's real nature and His real purpose. It is not the condition of a man who knows he is acting foolishly, but through procrastination puts off the reformation — that is one condition — but it is not Euphoria. It is the condition of a man who believes that he is so right and so safe that he has no need of reformation. Consequently he has no fear of sin, no foreboding about temptation and no sense of evil. Life becomes dangerously superficial and spiritually emasculated.

Biblical Examples

There are some Biblical examples of Euphoria. Luke 12:19 — the parable of the rich farmer. All was well — the house was palatial, the feeding was sumptuous, the bank balance was soaring; life was wonderful. There was nothing to be concerned about — "rest and take thine ease". There were other things, but they were invisible to this man. Overweight, out-of-breath, no exercise — his wife nagged him about his indifference to the rules, but he laughed her into silence in front of the servants. It was a lovely funeral — they said. Just as he would have liked, but it came a bit sooner than he really wanted.

Matthew 7:26 — the parable of the two builders. The sand was so smooth and so easy to work. Some interfering busybody said something about building rules but he was sent off with a short answer. Why make things harder than they need be? He was ever so happy — he had finished the work about the middle of August. He was able to sit in the garden and hear the brook babbling by. In December the babbling brook broke its banks — the breeze became a tempest. The Euphoria turned to terror. The house became a tomb. He was buried without any funeral arrangements.

Revelation 3:1 — the ecclesia at Sardis. The city was a place of immortality, loose living and luxury loving. It was a byword among the other cities. Life was easy, flabby and decadent. There was an ecclesia of God in Sardis and it was at peace. There was no heresy, no persecution, no Judaism, no problems. Everything was first rate. Although the surroundings were fraught with danger, everybody at

Sardis — well, nearly everybody — was well pleased with the spiritual condition of the meeting. They were at peace and at rest. It was peace by stagnation and the rest of death. They had a great name — it was said they were lively and good. They did not know the real truth about themselves, because the dead know not anything. That is the curse of Euphoria — and it ought greatly to be feared.

The tenth chapter of the first Letter to the Corinthians tells us about the people of God who were right in the heart of true religion and enjoying all the advantages of their special relationship with God. Verse 5 begins with an interesting word: "Howbeit . . ." It prepares us for the account of their failure, and in verse 12 the Apostle Paul reveals the root cause: "Wherefore let him that thinketh he standeth take heed lest he fall." Is there in the whole of the Bible a better sentence to describe the nature of Euphoria?

Fear and Confidence

Plainly Euphoria is the extreme opposite of depression and yet both conditions have a common identity — they are both eccentric — away from centre. It is right for believers to be optimistic about overcoming the forces of evil. It is right to have assurance about the power of God's word and prayer and fellowship in the fight against sin. It is utterly wrong to be optimistic when the sources of strength are neglected. It is utterly foolish to be assured when the assurance is rooted in the wrong things. So the middle and right position is a fear of the evil forces ranged against us — but without despair or depression, and with a hopeful confidence in those things which God has provided to enable those who are willing to hold fast at the centre of the faith.

About Euphoria there is one fleck of light. Usually the euphoric spirit discovers the truth sooner or later through some bitter experience or some awful failure which unveils the real condition. Thereafter the soul will come to itself. False confidence is shattered by a cold realisation of the facts. Boasting is seen to be bunkum. Complacency is crestfallen. The trumpet is muted. Standing jauntily gives way to heeding carefully. In the heeding are all those blessed forces which redress and repair the soul.

51

19

STRESS

STRESS is different from all the other maladies considered so far, inasmuch as the bodily condition and the spiritual counterpart are more closely connected and more strongly interdependent, than in most other cases. To put it plainly, bodily stress and spiritual stress are inextricably interwoven. Nearly always when the soul is suffering from tension it is because the powers of the mind and body are overstretched. Spiritual work often involves the use of bodily powers, and always the use of the mind. In these circumstances, when the body is worn and weary, so is the spirit. When the mind is distraught and distracted, spiritual exercise is a burden and a drag. So the disciple who is overworked and overwrought can rarely be overjoyed in the Truth.

In the worst experience of stress, the work of the Truth becomes a nuisance. Something which aggravates the anxiety and intensifies the pressure. It tightens the timetable of life; adds weight to the burden and irritation to the mind. The neglect of the Truth, which the stress enforces, introduces a feeling of guilt, which in turn adds to the general disability. Everything is done in a hurry, and the hurrying becomes harrowing. Even sleep is sleep without rest. Long days and short nights; to bed tired, from bed tired. Feeding is a habit more than a pleasure. The ringing telephone a jangle; visiting friends an interference. Family fellowship takes a cut. Playtime becomes "Not now" time. Eyes are sad and hearts are heavy. Stress is strain — strained too much. It is tension tightened to breaking point. It is pressure pushed beyond the safety limit. Too much work, too much worry, too much wear. It is back to the wall, cut off from retreat. It is holding the fort against impossible odds. Things postponed to gain relief become doubly oppressive at last. In the ups

52

and downs, through the sagging and the sighing, by the wearing and the tearing, usually the crucial element is time.

Very often stress can be identified as thirty hours of pressure in twenty four hours of time. In the end something has to give.

Redeeming the Time

Because of the nature of modern day living, never was there a period when time was so vital. When all is said and done living the life of faith is really the right use of time. Everybody has to do something with it. Indolent people waste it, busy people save it, bored people kill it, conductors beat it, musicians keep it, railway trains sometimes lose it — disciples are urged to redeem it. The reference is in the Ephesian letter, chapter 5, verses 15 and 16: "See then that ye walk circumspectly, not as fools, but as wise, redeeming the time, because the days are evil".

It may seem a strange word to use about time, but it is the right word because it means, Use it to the best advantage. It is a word out of the market place; make a good bargain, take the opportunity to do well. That is why Paul says "circumspectly, not as fools, but as wise". What makes the exhortation so relevant today is that never was there an age when so many time saving systems are in use, yet never was there an age with so little time to spare. The more time is saved the less time is available. Just one example: the writer remembers washing day when he was a boy; eight hours of coppers, mangles, tubs, dollies, suds of all kinds, and wet, wet clothes. Today, all finished in about three hours flat. It reflects the general trend in time saving. In the old days Sunday meeting travel involved say three hours of walking during the morning, afternoon and evening appointments. Today that three hours is thirty minutes in a car. Compared with the old days a great deal of time is being saved, but mysteriously, there is no time to spare.

If there is one phrase which characterises this age, it is the little phrase, "must dash". Constantly it falls from the lips of the saints, especially those in the grip of stress and strain. If the day comes that disciples have to give an account in detail of their lives before Christ the Judge, then the most likely explanation of failure will have to be that they did not have time to succeed.

Striking the Right Balance

The nature of today's society has forced this fact upon us; that living the life of faith faithfully means making the right use of our time. Never was there a period when this was so true. So when the Apostle Paul says, "not as fools, but as wise", the wisdom consists in striking a right balance in the use of time between the things of today and the things of eternity. Between the forces which are spiritual and those which are temporal. The teaching of the parable of the Unjust Steward is very applicable here. The purpose of its main teaching is fixed in one sentence in that parable:

"The children of this world are in their generation wiser than the children of light." (Luke 16:8)

Which means, if only the disciples of Christ would put into their religion the same devotion and persistence which the unbelievers put into their ordinary affairs.

Notice how people in the world with an objective, strive, slave, agonise, drive on and persist in the quest for success. The parable is saying — if only the children of light were as assiduous in the pursuit of their discipleship. So the point now to stress is simply this — a balance has to be struck between the claims of ordinary life and the claims of the life of faith, in order to live the Truth truly. Both groups of claims are legitimate and right, but the vital thing is to get them into proper perspective. That really is the meaning of "redeeming the time".

What Makes the Balance Right?

The use of the word redeem, that is using the opportunity to the very best advantage, is saying something very revealing about where the balance ought to be struck. It is not supposed to be a neat middle position where, like on a pair of scales, each side is about equal — nicely positioned and just evenly balanced. In this case the best advantage is strongly in favour of the cause of Christ, and therefore we have a paradox which tells us that the right balance means heavily weighted to one side. A balance between the things which are transient and the things which are eternal, and it is heavily weighted in favour of the eternal.

Of course this will come as no surprise, indeed it is what we might expect and in theory it is something we all approve. Everybody is strongly in favour of the eternal. This is especially true when the Truth is in jeopardy, or is being attacked and assaulted by hostile forces; when the principles of the Truth are in danger of being corrrupted and even destroyed. All good men and women in Christ will stand up and be counted. But how often does this happen?

The writer has been in the Truth nearly half a century and in that time twice only has he had to take a stand of this kind. Twice only has he had to say, "Here I stand and I will not be moved and I will take the consequences". If disciples wait for this kind of situation so that they can strike a balance in favour of the eternal, then they are likely to wait half a lifetime. No — the issues are about us every day — the transient things and the eternal things are in conflict every day, every week, every year.

Decisions in this conflict have to be made as an everyday experience of life. Proof that this is right can be found in the final words of that sentence about redeeming the time. It goes on "because the days are evil". The word *days* is important. It was a daily thing. The evil forces had to be faced every day. Of course, if anyone had told the people of Ephesus that they were living in evil days they would have laughed their heads off. The city was prosperous, bustling, busy, thriving and rich. But the Apostle Paul is telling us that there are conditions which are favourable to the advancement of temporal things which at the same time can be disadvantageous to the saints. So the point to notice here is that they were to redeem the time in the ordinary conditions of daily life in Ephesus — and the reason, because the days were evil. They were in the midst of forces which could waste and impair their opportunities for faithful living. So not some great crisis every twenty years — but the commonplace things of daily life.

Redeeming the time means therefore, not letting the opportunities slip by, unused and neglected. Take care that involvement in transient things is so strong and so intrusive that the eternal things have to be disregarded for lack of time. Of course in theory the Truth is at the top of the list of priorities, but very often in practice it has to take its place among a dozen other things jostling for position. Sometimes it comes out on top and sometimes it comes out down the list. From observation and experience this is the writer's measurement.

55

Never was there a period when time was so precious, and so overworked. Why is it that with so much time being saved compared with the old days, there is so little time to spare? It is no great mystery — today people are doing so many more things. The things which take up most of the time today in people's lives are 1. Jobs and careers; 2. Homes and family; 3. Geographical isolation. Add to this list time needed to serve the Truth actively — and unless there is a right balance struck then you have all the factors which could end in stress.

Examine the Timetable Carefully

Sometimes the writer detects signs of weariness among brethren and sisters because they are trying to fit in so much. Think of this situation. Both partners in a marriage are working. There is therefore less time to spare for the work of the home. It has to be done in time that hitherto was available for resting, or working in the Truth, or recreation. So the pressure builds up and something has to go. The stress becomes acute. Weariness sets in and conditions develop similar to those described in the first paragraph of this chapter. When something has to go, sometimes what actually goes is active service in the Truth.

People who used to come to the Bible Class, do not come any more because they are too tired or there is not time. The writer well understands this problem. He is not unsympathetic. Jobs today seem to be so demanding and often seem so stressful. In some professions, evening work has come to be almost normal. People have to drop out of pastoral work; other responsibilities have to be shed; minimum participation has to become the normal — because of lack of time, and the stress of life. For those who mean business about facing the problem and redeeming the time there is only one way. Examine life's timetable seriously. Be willing to stand up and be counted in the commonplace things of everyday living. If forces have invaded life and are robbing us of time which ought to be given to God — then be willing to be drastic in pursuit of the solution.

It may mean saying to the boss about overtime — yes, but never on a Wednesday. It may mean ending the association which is taking so much of your energy and time. It may mean relinquishing the ambition if it is crowding out other things more spiritual. It may mean recognising that the possession of things is, after all, not essential to the real life of faith. Peace with less is better than plenty with restlessness.

It is not easy and the writer knows it is a lot easier in retirement. Again, when jobs are precarious then independence is much more difficult. But the call is to look at it incisively. See if in some way the spiritual present is being lost because our time is taken up too much by the transient. Here is a suggestion to help the examination.

The Test of Heavenly Principles

When endeavouring to strike a balance between the transient and the eternal, there is a right place to be standing in order to take account of both worlds. The right place is from where we may flash upon the situation the teaching of the Lord Jesus Christ and his Apostles, and therefore bring it to the test of God's holy word of Truth. In other words, bring to bear upon it the principles of heaven. Earthly things measured by heavenly principles. This is what the New Testament writers always do. Of course you would expect them to bring heavenly principles to bear upon the great things of the Truth. The vital doctrines, the paramount issues, the forces at the spiritual centre of the faith. These things you would expect to be subject to the great principles of the Word of God. But the New Testament writers do it with the quite ordinary things as well — the commonplace things of the faith.

Think of some examples:

"Husbands, love your wives, even as Christ also loved the church and gave himself for it." (Ephesians 5:25)

The husband's love for his wife is thankfully commonplace, it is going on everywhere. Valuable but commonplace — but in the mind of Paul it is related to the one great atoning act of love for the redeemed.

"Exhort servants to be obedient to their own masters . . . that they may adorn the doctrine of God our Saviour in all things." (Titus 2:9 – 10)

Industrial relations are important but not something on the highest level of spiritual life, yet Paul takes time to measure it by a reference to the great fact of salvation.

"Masters, forbear threatening, knowing that your Master also is in heaven." (Ephesians 6:9)

A direction to employers upon how they should treat their employees — commonplace enough and yet Paul justifies it on the grounds that what they do will be judged by the one Master in heaven who is Lord of all.

Perhaps the very best example of this — the New Testament writers bringing great heavenly principles to bear upon ordinary things — is in 2 Corinthians chapter 8. This chapter is about something which some people would regard as the most commonplace thing of all — money. The chapter is about a collection for the poor saints at Jerusalem. It may well be commonplace but in certain circumstances it becomes ennobled. In 2 Corinthians 8 the Apostle Paul calls it *a grace*: "Therefore, as ye abound in every thing, in faith, and utterance, and knowledge, and in all diligence, and in your love to us, see that ye *abound in this grace also*" (verse 7).

So Paul calls the taking of a collection and the giving of money a grace. He is anxious that the Corinthians should give as generously as possible — he wants them to use this ordinary opportunity to help their deprived brethren and sisters as abundantly as they can. Notice how he does it: "For ye know the grace of our Lord Jesus Christ, that, though he was rich, yet for your sakes he became poor, that ye through his poverty might be rich" (verse 9).

He brings to bear upon the commonplace thing of giving money the great sacrifice of the Redeemer and his all embracing love for the undone. He relates the grace of giving to the central doctrines of the faith. He measures it by that life which was won out of death by the sacrifice of God's own Son when he became utterly poor to make many rich.

So when disciples under stress are striking a balance between the transitory and the eternal; when they are weighing up how they can re-arrange their lives so as to give more time and energy to his cause and less to their own — let them think of the great doctrines of the faith, and bring to bear upon the situation the solemn words of Jesus the Saviour. Think of what he has given for our sakes. When the call comes for loyal service to the Truth and the old man of the flesh says, "Spare thyself brother" or "Spare thyself sister"—which means let somebody else bear the burden and let somebody else take the responsibility—think that if Jesus had spared himself, then our plight would be utterly pitiable.

To those suffering under stress, pressured and weary, the real solution appears to be clear. Relieve the pressure and ease the stress by a sensible re-arrangement of the timetable. Be drastic, be courageous, be honest. Face the facts squarely. It may mean losing something of the things which moth and rust corrupt but it will mean gaining something which is incorruptible and undefiled. Remember that very often spiritual stress has its origin in bodily stress. Ease the earthly burden, take another look at the rat race, start to sleep well and enjoy your food. Take an occasional holiday. Play with the children. Greet your partner with a smile and a kiss. You may well feel that the world looks better — your world and God's world, and the Truth is something to be treasured and enjoyed.

20

DEHYDRATION

DEHYDRATION is an abnormal loss of fluid from the body and invariably the loss of fluid is accompanied by a loss of sodium chloride (salt). Sometimes there is also a loss of potassium and other chemical compounds, but salt is the substance which usually is lost in the greatest concentration, through loss of water. The effects of dehydration can be serious. The body is divided into different sections as far as body fluids are concerned and each section has a proper level of water and salt to function properly.

In a remarkable way, when this level is disturbed, the body works to re-establish the right level in each section by a rapid movement of water to correct any imbalance. As the chemical elements like sodium and potassium are necessary in different quantities in different sections, the process is complicated. When the loss of water is high and the compensating movement of fluid is insufficient to maintain the right balance, then the body cells become seriously dehydrated. If the condition is not treated, there results serious weight loss, as much as several pounds per day; then a burning thirst and difficulty in swallowing; the skin becomes dry and wrinkled and the eyes become shrunken. Eventually the pulse rate rises and the heart becomes inefficient. The kidneys cease to function properly and substances are retained in the body which should be eliminated and then pass into the blood stream. In its worst condition dehydration can result in heart attacks and serious renal failure — both of which may be fatal.

Treatment, obviously, must be designed to replace the lost water and the lost chemical substances. But the first essential is to discover what has caused the depletion of these elements. That is, the physical circumstances which have cut off the supply of water and salt, must be eliminated. As one medical authority has put it, ''The sailor or the desert traveller must be rescued, the vomiting infant must be cured and the underlying disease must be treated''. When this first cause has been corrected, then proper and measured amounts of water and salt can be given. Very soon the system will respond and gradually the correct levels will be restored to the different compartments of the body. This will result in a restoration of the complicated functions of the kidneys, the circulatory system and the purification of the blood stream. So by the application of water and salt there is health.

Spiritual Dehydration

The reader should have no difficulty in perceiving how dehydration can be a disease of the soul. The condition describes a life dried up, parched and withered. Lived to the full in one sense perhaps, and yet empty in the true sense of the spiritual meaning of that word. The wandering boy in the parable of Jesus filled his belly but he was really emaciated. It is a life of limitation and the boundary is fixed by the clamant cry of the flesh. The vision is short sighted. The experience is earthly only. It is life lived as though this were the only world. No ear for the sounds of eternity. A life mastered by appetite which no present satisfaction can quench. The demands of the flesh can be depraved, sensual, vulgar, but not always. Sometimes they are sophisticated and refined. There are choices high and there are choices low — but fundamentally they are on the same level — the craving of the flesh, which is never really satisfied. At the moment of achievement it is the one thing that matters, but afterwards the feeling of dry disappointment. Sometimes it involves the prostitution of the highest powers for the lowest purposes. Quickly enjoyed, then slowly despised. A dream fulfilled, a nightmare realised. The paradox of paradoxes. Busy, full, taking all and at last having nothing but thirst and hunger. It is like drinking sea water.

The power of the flesh unchecked drains the life of the very elements that were designed to make it good: faith, hope and love. These are the water of life. Paul puts it plainly — to live in the flesh is to mind the things of the flesh. Minding the things of the flesh

61

means consequently that the things of the spirit are neglected. The heart is hardened. The soul is a desert. Pursuing, possessing, pretending — life becomes like a dried up pool. Once a place of peace and pleasure, but now drained and deserted. This is life dehydrated. No upward look; no hope for tomorrow; no commerce with the Spirit; the destiny of dust.

Paul puts it plainly again — the mind of the flesh is death.

To the human mind there are gradations of fleshly life. Some are popular and approved, some are shocking and deplored, but to Paul the result is the same — the mind of the flesh is death. And it leads to death because the essential elements that make for spiritual living are drained away and not replaced. So at last a burning thirst which is never quenched; a vision which, rightly named, is blindness; a system of life poisoned by forces which should be shed but which instead are retained and absorbed.

So out of this drained condition a voice cries for help — in the words of the Psalmist, ''My loins are filled with burning''. It is the cry of a man dried and doomed by a bondage he has made for himself. It is the voice of a soul pining for some alleviation of a devouring hunger; a spirit disillusioned and disappointed. ''My loins are filled with burning, there is no soundness in my flesh''.

The Blessed Cure

The answer to this cry was heard first, a long time ago in the land of Israel, at a celebration of the Feast of Tabernacles. ''If any man thirst, let him come unto me and drink'' (John 7:37). The Apostle John tells us that this was the cry of Jesus on the last day of the Feast, that is the eighth day. It should be understood that these words were spoken circumstantially, that is out of the peculiar circumstances of the eighth day. Commentators tell us that during the seven days of the Feast of Tabernacles water was carried from the pool of Siloam or from the brook Kidron and it was poured out in the Temple to signify to the worshippers two things. First, that God had answered the need of water for their forefathers in the wilderness — it was real water to quench a real thirst. Second, to remind them that their Hebrew prophets had foretold of a day to come when rivers of waters would renew and remake the barren desert so that it would blossom as a rose, under the providential care of God; the real significance being the revival of the nation's spiritual life under the rule of their Messiah. The water of spiritual life for Israel.

But on the eighth day, the last day of the feast, *there was no carrying of the water at all,* and this was just as significant as the carrying of the water on the previous seven days. It was intended to remind the Hebrew worshippers that the great spiritual promise had not been fulfilled. Still they waited for the coming of the one who would give them the water which promised so much and which would renew their life. So, on the last day of the feast, when the men and women of Israel dwelt upon the lack of fulfilment, Jesus stood and cried saying, "If any man thirst, let him come unto *me* and drink". What he is saying is that all the sense of lack, all the realisation of unfulfilment, the burning thirst, the spiritual weakness, can be met and satisfied in him. He is a man with an essential remedy for an essential need and he cries out with the shout of God: "If any man thirst, let him come unto me".

Think who he is crying to. He is crying to a people broken with weariness, bereft through a threadbare religion, groping in the gloom, beset with failure, suffering from dehydration and longing for some relief.

Salt and Water

Are the words of the crying man true? If they are not then it is the cruellest deception ever perpetrated upon a suffering generation. But there are thousands upon thousands of witnesses who would testify that, put to the trial, the words are true. He is no charlatan, he is the life giver — this is what they say. They have found that when they were thirsty, tempest tossed and weary, finding nothing to slake their burning desire for some relief — through this crying man life's fitful fever was cooled. The unsuccoured life in the desert was changed. Water gushed from the rock — and they praised the Lord and drank and drank. The words are magnificently true and he deserves to be enthroned — now in the hearts of all who need the living water and one day soon in Zion, from whence shall flow the therapeutic grace for the healing of every ill and the ending of all agony, the full realisation of the life giver's goodness.

Let us never forget one thing. The water is living water because it has all the elements that make for spiritual health. Once the Man of

Nazareth said to his disciples, "Salt is good ... have salt in yourselves and be at peace one with another". Surely the implication is clear — that from him may be gathered that salt which is divinely good and by whose aseptic influence corruption is halted and purity is assured. So by the water and the salt, suffering men and women are relieved of dehydration and restored to the life of the Spirit.

21

AIDS

WE must remind ourselves that AIDS is an acronym for Acquired Immune Deficiency Syndrome. It is ironic that the word formed by the initials is in itself such a contradiction. AIDS aids nothing except the progress of disease and death. At the time of writing this chapter it is true that more people are dying of other diseases than of AIDS (at present two people die from it every day in Britain), but the important factor which makes the issue so different is that the infection is spreading unchecked and there is no known cure. In any disease where there is some proven treatment there is hope, but with this disease there is nothing. At present its progress is unabated. Add to that the complication that there is a seven year incubation period, which means that the infection is contracted and spread in utter ignorance for a long time. Another thing which makes the condition so serious is that the infection is passed on through forces which are among the most compulsive of human activities — sexual intercourse and drug taking.

AIDS on the attack

Some experts say that this disease could prove to be the worst pestilence ever to strike the modern world. They speak of ten million people being affected up to the present in some 85 countries. Acquired Immune Deficiency Syndrome is the professional way of indicating that the body's natural powers for fighting infection are rendered impotent and the immune response which is normally present in a healthy body is lost. It means the defences are destroyed and the body is exposed to every infection which normally would be harmless, but which with no defence, suddenly becomes deadly. So the observed effect is that people with AIDS become ill easily with diseases which ordinarily they would throw off, and in about two years they are dead.

But sadly the effect is not only the disappearance of the defences. The virus which causes AIDS is itself capable of introducing serious disease, particularly of the brain. What other deadly effect it may have upon the human constitution is something yet perhaps to be discovered by those who sadly are victims of this pestilential plague in today's society.

The condition is spread in several ways but the commonest is through sexual intercourse. Of course it should be understood that not every one with AIDS has been infected by that means.

Leaving aside the causes of its proliferation, the thing to realise is that those who are suffering from the disease need every help and succour. When someone is dying from an incurable condition, a lecture on morality brings little comfort and provokes no worthwhile resolution. Imposed isolation is the last thing you want when you already feel isolated. Those who minister to AIDS sufferers deserve encouragement and support. As things are at present they can bring nothing by way of treatment for the healing of the disease, but plenty by way of care, comfort and consolation.

It may be that if time goes on a vaccine will be produced which will prove effective in the prevention of the disease, or perhaps a drug for its cure. But from available information this is not likely to happen for some time. Some experts predict it may be fifteen years before the materials have been discovered, tested and approved. Some people are deeply worried by the danger and the prospect; others are dismissive and indifferent. Surely nobody in their right mind should treat lightly so serious a situation; an infectious deadly disease with no cure and no method of containment. The common sense of self preservation should teach all people everywhere to avoid the occasions which introduce the risk of infection. But human nature being what it is, who dare be optimistic that universal sanity will prevail? The best hope is that soon the worldwide research will be successful and a cure will be found and prevention will be possible.

AIDS in the soul

We come now to the pointed, pertinent question — what is the spiritual counterpart of AIDS? What condition in the soul's experience is the equivalent of this awful disease which renders the recuperative powers inactive and exposes the system to a multitude of hostile infections — sinister and destructive? Here is a proposal — the spiritual counterpart is despair, rooted in unbelief. Consider it carefully.

Despair at its worst refuses every means of grace, rejects every possibility of improvement or change, denies every chance of recovery. So all the forces which, given use, could cure the condition are rendered impotent. The powers which could revive the spirit, recover the lost ground and create an optimistic atmosphere, are blocked and prevented. So the powers of recuperation are halted by the barricades of despair. Thus the soul, unshielded and like a wound twice sore, is exposed to every new pressure, aggravated by every fresh doubt, descends and droops more deeply into hopelessness.

In that condition, the element of unbelief fixes the hopelessness relentlessly. While it persists the soul and spirit are in a strait jacket of spiritual impotence. So despond and gloom have free course. Misjudgment and miscalculation abound. A condition of darkness through which no sympathy can break. The best acts of love are rejected. Even angels would be under suspicion. Think how awful it is — to believe that you are in the dreary universe alone. No immortality; no control; no hope. Behind the cloud no silver lining. The wind is chill. Reading, praying, serving — all in the past tense.

The condition has been fixed by the psalmist in Psalm 4 in one sad sentence: "Who will show us any good?" It is not the Psalmist's word, he is quoting the word of the man mastered by despair. Its cause is not some adversity or the pressure of disadvantageous circumstances. This kind of despair has its origin independent of circumstances, in an underlying malady of human life — unbelief. In this frame of mind the Word of God is never read; the pathway of prayer is abandoned; the fellowship of saints is spurned. The contention of the unbelieving mind is that in these things there is no good. The Word of God is no good; prayer is no good; fellowship is no good. "Who will show us *any* good?" Men denying God lose the key to goodness. The awful tragedy of this condition is that those in it are self isolated from all the forces which could bring relief and restoration.

If a man is suffering from a deadly disease and refuses point blank to avail himself of the certain remedy, it could be said he died of the disease. But it could also be said he died by his own will. A kind of suicide. People who commit suicide usually have no faith in the alternative. They cannot believe that living is better. Cannot is the important word, because it proposes a kind of impotence, arising from unbelief. This is precisely what is alleged in Hebrews 3:19, "They *could not* enter in because of unbelief". That takes us to a place we have been already in these chapters — the people of God on the margin of the good land at Kadesh Barnea. The record is in Numbers chapter 13.

In preparation for taking the new land they resolved to send in spies to weigh up the situation. One of the first recorded acts of espionage in the old world. So they went in secretly, did their work and came back with their reports. The word is used in the plural form because there were two — a majority report and a minority report. In most respects they were identical — it was in the conclusion that they differed. In effect the reports went like this — "It is a good land, it flows with milk and honey, the fruit is luscious and the land is fertile". It was at this point that the reports diverged.

The majority report went on to say, "But there are giants and there are walled cities and the people are very strong — it will be too much for us. We had better not go, let us make a captain and go back to Egypt". The minority report said, "It is true there are walled cities and the people are strong and there are giants, but the Lord our God will lead us into this land and give us possession — let us go up and take it". The majority report prevailed and the Hebrew man says it did so because of unbelief. It is so extraordinary as to be almost unbelievable.

They said because there are difficulties we have no help. Remember, this was just a little while after they had been rescued from Egypt with masterly power by God. They had seen all the power and hostility of Egypt defeated by one man, their leader, wielding a rod — the rod of God. But just think of their deliverance through the Red Sea. Of all the miracles in the Bible it is the most spectacular, because it was so unique and so public. Let the reader imagine taking a stand upon the coast and looking out to sea, and then to imagine the sea parting and standing firm, and the opening of a road there through the very depths of the ocean. To our human minds it is unthinkable — it is beyond conception. To witness such a thing would be so aweful as to make it impossible ever to forget. It would fill us with reverent fear for all time. The thing to remember is this — *these people had seen it*. Not just as bystanders but they had experienced it, because by it they were delivered finally from Egypt, and had seen their enemies swallowed up in the raging waves and the roaring foam. Who could ever forget such a thing?

Yet here is the mystery — when they contemplated the walled cities of Canaan and when they remembered the giants and the supposed strength of the Canaanites — their minds went blank. When the proposers of the minority report said that the Lord God was with them and would keep His promise to give them possession — they could not remember anything to give them conviction. All that happened through the Red Sea was never mentioned — and never remembered. See then why it is unbelievable — there is about this something mysterious.

It is telling us something about the awful effect of unbelief. Observe a kind of impotence once they rejected trust in God. Yet what they could remember so well was Egypt — not the slavery and the bondage and the persecution, but the leeks and the onions and the garlic. People obsessed with the material and utterly blind to the spiritual. No wonder the Hebrew man was so categoric — they *could* not . . .

What makes it so interesting is that in the Bible so often hope and trust for the future is generated by remembrance of the past. Past experience predicates trust for what lies ahead. He who has saved in the past will be able to save again. He who led then is able to lead again. This is how David was sustained when his faith was being assaulted by his enemies. ''Why art thou cast down, O my soul? and why art thou disquieted within me? . . . therefore will I remember thee from the land of Jordan, and of the Hermonites, from the hill Mizar'' (Psalm 42:11,6). David's faith was strengthened when he fell back on what had happened at Jordan, Hermon and Mizar.

This should have happened at Kadesh Barnea, but mysteriously there was no recollection of anything in the past but the fleshpots of Egypt. Amnesia brought on by unbelief. The sad end of the story is that all those who refused to enter the good land trustfully — that is those who supported the majority report — never entered it at all but were lost in the wilderness. It happened because all the forces that could have led them and kept them and saved them, were rejected.

Their actual words are a revelation: "Would God that we had died in the land of Egypt! or would God we had died in this wilderness! wherefore hath the Lord brought us into this land, to fall by the sword, that our wives and our children should be a prey? Were it not better for us to return into Egypt? . . . Let us make a captain, and let us return into Egypt" (Numbers 14:2 – 4). This is another way of saying, "Who will show us any good?"

The supporters of the minority report tried urgently to change the mind of the doubters — they said: "The land, which we passed through to search it, is an exceedingly good land. If the Lord delight in us, then he will bring us into this land, and give it us; a land which floweth with milk and honey. Only rebel not ye against the Lord, neither fear ye the people of the land; for they are bread for us: their defence is departed from them, and the Lord is with us: fear them not" (Numbers 14:7 – 9).

It was sane and sensible and faithful — but it was rejected by the unbelievers, and most violently, for it says that the congregation bade stone them with stones. This is a classic example of despair rooted in unbelief. The despair is focused in the cry, "Would God we had died in Egypt", and the unbelief in, "We are not able to . . ."

So all the forces which could have led them safely and established them securely and satisfied them joyfully — were rejected and nothing could change it. They were resolved upon failure. Now spiritual AIDS is like this. Despair rooted in unbelief which results in rejection of all the powers of recovery and renewal — so the soul is exposed to the insidious powers of doubt and denial, hopeless and restless. Tempest tossed and weary, nothing is any good.

Now think of recovery. With bodily AIDS so far this is not possible — but thank God with spiritual AIDS there is hope. It is possible to be made whole. But in this case, as in others, prevention is better than cure. The important thing is to watch out for the early symptoms and for the conditions which foster the disease.

For example — looking at life in little bits instead of the broad sweep of God's purpose. Thinking we know better than the wisdom of God's Word. Fear of some deprivation as a result of keeping true.

Fear of doing without some comfort, which we cannot bring ourselves to relinquish in Christ's cause. The wooing winsomeness of some material advantage which has the effect of sapping our courage. Some association outside the Truth which weakens our resolve. Not being able to let go the one thing which Christ cannot allow us to retain on the pilgrimage. These are the things about which disciples have to be vigilant. Unchecked and unchallenged they could lead on to holding the Truth with light hands and might ensnare the unwary into some kind of doubt and despair which is dangerous and paralysing.

So prevention is better than cure every time. But supposing that a cure is the only solution — what then? There is an important difference between bodily AIDS and spiritual AIDS which must be noted. People with the bodily disease desperately want to be cured — but the people with the spiritual disease often do not. If the sufferer refuses point blank to receive any assistance of any kind by way of recovery then the only thing is to pray for help and guidance and trust in God.

But supposing the sufferer *is* willing to receive some kind of communication, then here is something to ponder. It must be evident that in a severe case of despair and unbelief, in some way faith has got to be restored. Without this a cure is impossible. Now when all the speculation is over and when all the arguments have been ventilated, the Bible has one thing to say categorically about the acquisition of faith — it "cometh by hearing, and hearing by the word of God" (Romans 10:17). So somehow the sufferer has got to be persuaded to get back to the Word of God.

Here is one way of endeavouring to achieve that — the writer is not saying it is the only way, but it is one way worth trying. That phrase, "So then faith cometh by hearing", in the Authorised Version is translated in the New English Bible like this: "We conclude that faith is awakened by the message". That states the objective precisely — it is an awakening.

First of all consider this — the Hebrew man who said "they could not enter in because of unbelief" was sending his letter to people who were very much in a condition like those at Kadesh Barnea. They were turning back from their high destiny. They were denying what previously they had received gladly. They were on the verge of apostasy. They were saying in effect, Who will show us any good?

So what he is saying to them in an attempt to effect their recovery must be of great interest to us — because his problem was very much like our problem. By some means to awaken faith in those who previously had believed but now were in utter unbelief. Notice his method — take three passages and mark them well.

> *"Take heed, brethren, lest there be in any of you an evil heart of unbelief, in departing from the living God. But exhort one another daily, while it is called Today; lest any of you be hardened through the deceitfulness of sin. For we are made partakers of Christ, if we hold the beginning of our confidence stedfast unto the end."*
>
> (Hebrews 3:12 – 14)

In that passage fix on one word — *"confidence"*.

> *"That ye be not slothful, but followers of them who through faith and patience inherit the promises."*   (Hebrews 6:12)

In that sentence fix on *"be not slothful . . . but patient"*.

In the Bible the word patience does not just mean the ability to be calm and to keep your temper. It means more the ability to keep going, to endure, to persist. James says, "Ye have heard of the patience of Job". Now Job was not a particularly patient man in the popular meaning of the word, in fact he was quite exasperated with his friends during their wordy discourses. Job was a patient man in the sense that he hung on, in spite of his awful disabilities, and at last he triumphed as a man of great faith.

> *"Let us draw near with a true heart in full assurance of faith, having our hearts sprinkled from an evil conscience, and our bodies washed with pure water."*   (Hebrews 10:22)

In that passage select the words *"with a true heart"*.

Now take the selected words and put them together thus: "With confidence, not slothful but patient, but with a true heart." Now this is the process which somehow has to be followed for the shedding of unbelief and recovery of faith. Now the next thing is to say to the sufferer, Although you do not believe in this Word of God any more, will you, just for putting to the test this proposal, act for a little while as though you did believe in it slightly. Will you

72

venture just a little bit by being willing to read a little every day? In this matter nothing will be achieved unless you venture — be it ever so little. We understand that you do not have any trust in it — yes, we understand that, but be daring, be willing to experiment, even if it is only slightly. After all, people often read things in which they do not believe, or about which they have opposite opinions, just for the interest of it. So it is not inconsistent to venture in this way. And do it with patience, that is, do it every day and do not be put off. Be persistent and hold on to the process, even if you doubt its usefulness — give it a chance. And as far as you can, try to do it with a true heart — that is, do it as somebody who really wants to find the truth if the truth can be found.

We have sympathy with your despair and we know your doubt is well fixed, but surely doing something positive is better than doing nothing at all. We know that in the end belief is a very personal thing and one man's faith is not sufficient for two, but we want to encourage you and we will come and join with you regularly if you would like it so. You said you were not sure — well, that is a step forward. The worst condition is being too cocksure. Sometimes uncertainty has promise if it is willing to venture. We would love to stay with you in this adventure and perhaps together we can find a chink of light. Somehow together we have to gain the assurance of things hoped for and prove the reality of things unseen.

So step onward, never mind how tentatively, and walk with a bit of confidence — you might find that you have put your foot upon a bit of rock and if you do, move on from there. And as you do it, try to speak these words and never mind how falteringly you say them — "Lord, help thou mine unbelief".

The writer claims no credit for the invention of this process. Indeed, first of all it is in the Word of God but the exposition of it he first met years ago when he was young, in the works of a Bible expositor of the old school and to whom for the understanding of it he is sincerely grateful. About it, this can be said. It does work. There have been those who followed it and who out of awful doubt and despair came to absolute certainty about God and His purpose and as a result refused any longer to put upon their own lives the measurement of dust and doom, but squared their way of life anew with the commandments of the Living God, and looked forward

73

with hope and confidence to the coming of His kingdom upon the earth and the enthronement of His anointed King, and to life everlasting.

Bodily AIDS seems to be a new disease, but spiritual AIDS is as old as human nature. Whether the cure for bodily AIDS will be found this side of the Kingdom of God, who can tell? But the cure for spiritual AIDS is revealed and known and is proven. It is well expressed by the words of Psalm 107: ''He sent his word, and healed them, and delivered them from their destructions'' (verse 20).

Thank God He did and does for those who are willing.

22

SCHIZOPHRENIA

THE writer recollects a piece of graffiti from years ago: "You will never walk alone with schizophrenia". That describes certain aspects of it very well. Some kinds of schizophrenia do produce a condition which manifests two quite different personalities in the same person. Of course the medical definition is more clinical. First of all the word schizophrenia means literally "splitting of the mind", and the idea of the split mind comes from the fact that there are times of mental normality and times of mental abnormality in the same personality. The abnormal symptoms are hallucinations, shallow emotional responses, bizarre behaviour, unrealistic and illogical thinking, and false beliefs and illusions. Sometimes these abnormal symptoms are circumstantial and with a change of circumstances there is a return to normality. Where this disease differs from other mental illness is that the condition is not continuous but intermittent. The personality is at one time gentle, kind and sympathetic — then suddenly harsh, violent and accusatory. What appears to be two different people in the same person. That this is true was once proven to the writer when he had the opportunity to observe over several years a patient suffering from schizophrenia — one day Doctor Jekyll, the next day Mr. Hyde.

On a point of accuracy, it must be recognised that there are other symptoms and other kinds of mental disturbance than those mentioned here which accompany schizophrenia, but they cannot concern us now. Those chosen here are selected to stress the element of the split mind and the dual personality which is part of this distressing condition.

The Treatment

Treatment seeks to provide both prevention and cure. It goes almost without saying that where there might be a predisposition towards some form of mental strain, then it is important to avoid the influences which might aggravate it. In addition, there is the need to live in accordance with rules of health which are sensible and prudent, bearing in mind the forces which can impair mental wellbeing, if not resisted. To put it in plain terms — there is a clear need for obedience to the rules of good health. Psychic stress and emotional upsets are to be carefully avoided and self control and self denial are to be carefully encouraged.

A cure is now a possibility, with the modern methods of treatment. The old methods of straight jackets and solitary confinement have been superseded by more carefully selective treatment, like occupational therapy and home treatment which includes fresh air, good food, sound sleep and the control of excitement. Sometimes schizophrenia may require institutional treatment, but the modern tendency is to get the patient out of detention into everyday life, at work and enjoying recreation and exercise. In short, to live life under conditions as normal as possible, with the influence of care and kindness, and where necessary under the discipline of firmness and sound guidance. The reports of improvement under this system include a sound pattern of sleep, increase of body weight and physical strength, a diminution of delusions, and sometimes a complete disappearance of abnormality, conduct no longer eccentric and attitudes which reveal a proper rationality and balanced judgement. Plainly, a real desire to get well and keep well. So the cure of schizophrenia is achieved.

Spiritual Schizophrenia

The reader should have no difficulty in discerning the spiritual counterpart of mental schizophrenia. Life is made up of a split personality — one part manifesting the signs of true discipleship and the other secretly in submission to the flesh. One part full of the Truth, another part doing the very things which deny the Truth. Dr. Jekyll, the disciple and Mr. Hyde, the rebel. It is at this point that great care has to be exercised in forming conclusions. It must be recognised that there is in every disciple something of a split personality; that is to say there are two natures, the old man of the flesh and the new man of the spirit. Because the desires of the flesh can never be made spiritual, there is an unchanging conflict between the one and the other.

The Apostle Paul bears testimony to the truth of this situation in Romans chapter 7:

"For we know that the law is spiritual: but I am carnal, sold under sin. For that which I do I allow not: for what I would, that do I not; but what I hate, that do I. If then I do that which I would not, I consent unto the law that it is good. Now then it is no more I that do it, but sin that dwelleth in me. For I know that in me (that is, in my flesh,) dwelleth no good thing: for to will is present with me; but how to perform that which is good I find not. For the good that I would I do not: but the evil which I would not, that I do. Now if I do that I would not, it is no more I that do it, but sin that dwelleth in me. I find then a law, that, when I would do good, evil is present with me. For I delight in the law of God after the inward man: but I see another law in my members, warring against the law of my mind, and bringing me into captivity to the law of sin which is in my members." (verses 14 – 23).

This conflict which Paul describes in the life of the disciple is due to the characteristics of the two natures in the one person. The old nature is earthy and cannot please God; it profiteth nothing and in it dwelleth no good thing. As we have seen, all this is the language of the New Testament.

On the other hand, the new nature is created by God; it is called the New Man; it is described as spirit and it cannot be changed. It is the inward man and is renewed day by day. It is called newness of life and by it Christ dwells in the heart of the believer and through it the disciple strives for holiness. It is therefore inevitable that in the one personality there is bound to be conflict. This ought not to be the cause of disappointment or perplexity. Once the true situation is properly discerned, it can be faced with understanding and quiet confidence. Remember that Romans chapter 7 ends like this in response to a cry for help: "I thank God through Jesus Christ our Lord." All this brings us back to the need for carefulness when forming conclusions. Every disciple is aware of this conflict in the one personality but that does not mean that every disciple who is aware of the conflict is therefore suffering from spiritual schizophrenia. That is something different.

The Real Schizophrenia

This condition is one in which the 'I' of Romans chapter 7 is trying to sustain both natures in equal strength. The new nature is fostered and yet at the same time the old nature is fed. If it be thought this is impossible, then the writer, in spite of any theological theory, must say he has known it to happen. Think of this situation — a man is engaged in preaching the Truth, competently, regularly and sincerely. He desires genuinely to convert the unsaved. He is glad when others respond to his efforts. Or this — he is someone who finds the elucidation of prophecy an exciting enterprise; he will argue for this solution or that and is ready to defend well established interpretations. Or this — pastoral work gives him great satisfaction. He is glad to bring comfort to the sick and succour to the unprotected. If material help is needed for the needy he can be generous. If a hard decision has to be made affecting another disciple, then he tends to be easy going and sympathetic. On his own admission he is soft hearted. As far as assemblies are concerned, he is loyal and regular. This is one side of his personality.

The other side is different. It is secret, that is, it is secret to those who are not supposed to know. This side of the personality is flesh dominated. There is a strong appetite for some fleshly indulgence which is not resisted and is not denied. Instead it is fed and satisfied. It is not a case of a soul falling into failure through weakness; fighting against temptation and yet being submerged by the very strength of the enticement. Wanting to resist but sadly overwhelmed and beaten. A failure, reluctantly. No, this case is different, this schizophrenia. It is a case of the vision being shut to the visible; the hearing stopped to the voice of the spirit; the mind closed to the eternities. For the time being the flesh is first and last; mental, physical, sexual. Provocation is welcome; its occasions are sought out and enjoyed. Impediments to enjoyment are deplored; reforms are resisted and interference is resented. Vulgar or refined, the appetite has to be satisfied. For the time being there is no other world than this world. Indulgence is the object of living, the consuming consciousness of life. Faith is no matter; hope is forgotten; the only love is the love of self.

78

This is one part of the split personality. It exists in a mysterious way detached from the other part and unaffected by it. If it be argued that the condition as presented here is so bizarre as to be utterly incredible, then apply this test. Go back and re-read the paragraphs that describe the two parts of the split personality and then ask this question: Is there anything in the bad part which would on a practical level prevent the things of the good part being performed? For example, is it not quite possible for someone to indulge his fleshly passions and at the same time be a very generous person in time of need. The two urges are not incompatible. It is not impossible to preach well on the one hand and secretly to be impure on the other. Remember that the mind of the flesh is not subject to the law of God. This condition is rare but it is not impossible. It is a serious disease of the soul. The difference between one condition and the other is the difference between divinity and dust; between bondage and freedom; between life and death. That is why the situation is so stark and why those few who might be in it need help so badly. Schizophrenia may be rare but it is very serious.

The Treatment and the Help

The treatment entails a realisation on the part of the patient that life in the flesh, even with all its fleshly satisfaction, is really life only half realised. It is life without real thought. It is something less than life at its best. In the end it is corruption, it is bondage, it is prison, it is servitude. Lust is never really satisfied. Somehow the satisfaction is always deteriorating — next time more and more is demanded.

The things of fleeting time can never match the surging claims of the new man. The search at last must always end in hopeless dissatisfaction. So the first thing is to get the split mind, somehow, to come to terms with this inexorable fact. In other words, get rid of the delusions. He will need help, guidance and rebuke. In the end he must be helped to help himself. He must somehow be forced to face the truth. Lust degenerating is life doomed. All the things of the new life are spoiled, wasted, made naked, lost. The delusion that the two ways can live together successfully must be exposed. This marriage is impossible. Once he is convicted of this there is hope. Every encouragement must be given to avoid the occasions of the flesh bound life — and instead the rules of good health must be substituted.

79

It is easy to write it, but it is hard to perform. Obedience is the essential thing, obedience to the laws of life. Good food, pure water, the right atmosphere all have powerful influences — ask any reformed schizophrenic. One thing is certain — anything which feeds and sustains the new man, brings stronger control over the old man. People who feed upon the Word of God are most likely to make the flesh a servant and not a master. To the Galatians the message was so clear: ''Walk according to the spirit and the lust of the flesh ye shall in no wise fulfil'' (5:16). Another certainty is this — solitary confinement is no great help — loving fellowship is excellent. Warm, fruit-bearing friendship will do wonders. Well, it makes sense — anyone with a fleshbound past is sure to feel isolated when they come out into the light. What they need is kindness, sympathy and encouragement.

Then home treatment, free from spiritual stress, but full of spiritual inspiration, is something to be used and fostered on the pathway to recovery. The disciple who is good at home has started in the best place. Occupational therapy — this in spiritual terms means getting together with others in some activity in the cause of Christ. There is nothing like work with others to restore self respect. The fellowship of labour has therapeutic power. Then this — get the patient to forget the past. Brooding over wasted years will do nothing for the years ahead. If God has promised to forget why should His repenting children insist on doing the opposite? Brooding is harmful and can be dangerous. Things of the past should never be allowed to become obstacles for the future, and they can be if they are resurrected and given morbid re-enactment. So urge the patient to forget.

The thing to *remember* is this. Confronted by the Redeemer's promise, nothing is impossible: ''Whosoever cometh unto me I will in no wise cast out''. Mark this — *in no wise*. Under the discipline of his patient grace, the split mind can be healed. The new man reigns, the old man is subject. This is life in focus and in balance. The equilibrium of the Spirit.

80

23

BRADYCARDIA

BRADYCARDIA is a medical term to describe a slow beating heart. Care must be taken here. Not everyone with a slow beating heart has bradycardia. There are some people who have a slow heart naturally. Very often athletes come in this category. In such a case the heart beats slowly, but strongly and in rhythm and therefore efficiently. Bradycardia is where the slowness is due to some malfunction of the beat system. Usually this is a sluggishness in the electrical impulses which drive and control the heart beat. There are people with the opposite problem, where the electrical impulses are too lively and they suffer from a rapid heartbeat. This condition is called tachycardia. It does show how important it is that the conducting mechanism of the heart is right so that it works properly and efficiently. When the heartbeat is slow it results in a feeling of lassitude and weakness and may bring on fainting and blackouts. There is nearly always an attitude of lethargy due to the poor circulation of blood to the organs of the body. The patient feels he has no strength and therefore makes no effort because to do so is a real struggle. He feels weighed down and constricted through lack of strength. Because the heart is slow the inclination is slow. It is all part of bradycardia.

The treatment is to prescribe drugs which have the effect of increasing the heart beat which consequently improve the circulation and therefore make the system more efficient. The other treatment is to fit a pacemaker, which is designed, as its name suggests, to regulate the pace of the heartbeat and in the case of bradycardia to increase it to a sound and efficient pumping action. There are many people today who have pacemakers fitted and they lead active and busy lives, satisfying and enjoyable.

Bradycardia of the Soul

This condition could be described as spiritual slowness of heart. The symptoms are loss of passion, a feeling of spiritual lassitude, and even fainting. In the face of the need for faithful service, there is lethargy and lack of interest. What at one time was inspiring and well worthwhile is now seen as hardly worth bothering with. What used to excite now seems dull and sometimes boring. The old things, heard so often, make no appeal. Sometimes, the feeling is focused in a complaint that the meetings provide nothing to help. Either too dull or too lively. Sometimes too long or too short. Too involved or too simple. When friends show interest in the Truth, it is not encouraged, but passed on to others to follow up and develop.

It is a strange thing — this bradycardia. It is not loss of belief. Those who suffer from it have not come to the conclusion that the Bible is wrong or that their understanding of it is misguided and faulty. It is that now they have no enthusiasm for it. They are listless and without spiritual energy. If they speak of the Truth it is always about what it used to be like. They remember the days in the past when they were active and keen. They tell how once they worked in the Sunday School or in the pastoral care of the ecclesia. They had a Bible Study group in the home and it worked well. Sighing, they tell what it used to be like in their early days. Provoked, they might even tell how they used to be excited at meetings when the Truth was preached. They loved to hear about the signs that the Lord's coming was near. But now the excitement has gone. There is no passion. The meetings are neglected. They come but occasionally, and then are reluctant to stay to talk. Fellowship is not in favour. Detachment is a defence. Once they hurried in the cause of Christ, drawn onward by the noble prospect. Now the feet are shackled by lack of vision and loss of fervour. Pessimism where there used to be promise and possibility. The spirit is never amazed, the soul is never aflame, the heart never throbs.

A Real Case

In the New Testament there is a real life case of spiritual brady-cardia. It is in Luke chapter 24 — true, it is temporary but it is real enough. Two disciples are going home in the evening. They are walking out of Jerusalem to Emmaus where they live. They are not hurrying, indeed they are sauntering. Well, there is nothing to hurry about.

They are disappointed. The one they had hoped would redeem and reign over Israel had been executed. Their confidence was gone. Their passion had dried up. He had not been equal to the forces which were against him. As they walk they talk about what it had been like before. Remember he was a great prophet, his words and his deeds were mighty. They remember how fervent and excited they used to be.

The fire that used to blaze is now a few embers just glowing. That is why they are sauntering. There is nothing to do now. It started so well — now it is ending so sadly.

The diagnosis of their trouble is not left to our speculation. The supreme physician joined them on the Emmaus road. They did not recognise him because their eyes were holden that they should not know him. He asks them why they are walking and talking so sadly and so hopelessly. So they tell him of their dashed hopes, their lost expectations, their agonised disappointment.

Let us mark their actual words carefully because it reveals that their lives were in the past tense. They say about Jesus of Nazareth ''which *was* a prophet, mighty in deed and word before God and the people''. Again they say: ''But we trusted that it *had been he which should have redeemed Israel*''.

Let us not mistake it. They are not saying he was a fraud. They are not charging him with deception. They are not saying anything bad about him. They believe he was the best man they had ever known. What he tried for was something that filled their hearts with a new hope. At one time they were bubbling over with it — they loved and longed for it. Yes, he was a prophet and we had hoped . . . Oh yes, they loved his memory. How good it once had been. The geographical position is like a parable. They are leaving Jerusalem, the city of the Great King, to return to things as they used to be. To Emmaus, where life is ordinary and commonplace and as it was before. A return to the status quo, before the vision came. In reply to their confession of disappointment the physician diagnoses the trouble: ''O fools, and *slow of heart* to believe all that the prophets have spoken!''

That was the trouble then — heart slowness. If the spiritual pulse rate had been right they would have understood and would not have lost hope, but instead would have been invigorated by the very things which had disappointed them. They would have received with joy the testimony of the women that the tomb was empty and angels had proclaimed he was alive. Heart slowness had impeded their faith. Oh, let us not criticise them for this — how do we know if we would have been any more perceptive?

The record tells what happened: ''And beginning at Moses and all the prophets, he expounded unto them in all the scriptures the things concerning himself!'' Jerusalem to Emmaus is not a long journey, about 7 miles — so even sauntering it was not a long walk. Jesus joined them at some time along the route and in that short time revealed to them in the first five books of the Bible and then in all the prophets the things which showed what the Messiah was to be like and what he was to do.

What he said was not extra-Biblical. He did not add to what was written, but he took what was written and made it live. He gave them a new understanding of things which they had heard before many times and which had been part of their Hebrew education. Old things made new. The same things old and new. What a wonderful exposition it must have been. The Son of God opening the scriptures to two astounded disciples — on the road home and as the sun was westering.

That was the treatment designed and applied by the man who bore our sicknesses. The effect is told by the disciples after the stranger has been identified in breaking bread and has disappeared. They said one to another, ''Did not our heart burn within us, while he talked with us by the way, and while he opened to us the scriptures?'' Hearts that burn tend to beat faster. The new pulse rate resulted in action, in the same hour. No waiting to straighten things out, no delay to talk it over, no holding back until the morning. In the same hour they were on the way to Jerusalem at the double. They sauntered outwards, they went back hurrying. In this case the slow heart was a temporary condition soon cured because the remedy was wonderfully to hand.

The fire was low — but it has been written of the Messiah that he will not quench the smoking flax. That means not only will he not quench it, he will fan it into flame. Remember one thing for certain

— the cure was made sure when they were listening to him. It was not when they were talking to themselves, not when they were telling of their own sadness and their disappointment. The record goes out of its way to tell us when the cure took effect: ''Did not our heart burn within us, *while he talked with us by the way,* and while he opened to us the scriptures.''

The condition of spiritual bradycardia is put right by the impact of the Word of God. It might be some startling insight into its meaning, hitherto never seen. It might be some remarkable fulfilment of its promise, or its prediction suddenly realised. On the other hand it is sometimes achieved by a patient urging of another soul towards the slow hearted one — urging a return to the words of the love impulsed Saviour. Urge the patient to listen for the Imperial voice, that is able to make slow hearts throb with new hope. After all is said and done, the slow heart condition is a miserable and forlorn one. No real hope, no inspiration, no passion. Spiritually it is dull and dismal and blighted. Let the bringer of help emphasise that the doubt mastered life is wasted. Getting rid of it will be like a release from bondage; a healing of wounds; a flinging back of the shutters into an old vision made new and exciting. It is not just a matter of reading and marking and analysing. It is the impact of the person of the Emmaus Christ upon the listless soul. Let not the remedy turn into a vague generalisation. It must be personal, realistic, incisive. The shame of past failure ended; the exaltation of a new endeavour, faith inspired, making the heart strong and steady.

So, on a strictly practical level, never be willing to accept spiritual heart slowness as something which just has to be endured and cannot be cured. There are people who once were in this condition who now have burning hearts and shining faces in the service of the redeemer. Since part of the effect of the condition is a feeling of fainting, one word of the redeemer is paramount: ''Men ought always to pray and not to faint.'' Try to pray with the one who needs help — however reluctant they may be at first, keep trying. Use every means possible to bring them closer to the word of life. Talk to them about the need of others, to prove they are not uniquely exceptional. Show how it is possible to have a full-blooded, robust and exciting life of discipleship. If they are afraid because of their weakness, admit that a recognition of weakness is wholesome, but it is out of the very condition of weakness that Christ can restore and make strong. After all he did say: ''My strength is made perfect in your weakness.'' Luke 24 is telling us that Christ Jesus is very close to the weak and the disappointed. He is able to take the little that remains and make it throb with new hope and expectation.

God has a pacemaker for the slow hearted — if they will receive it.

24

LEPROSY (so-called)

WHY 'so-called'? Because it is certain that the disease known today as leprosy (infection with *Mycobacterium leprae*) is not the disease referred to in the Bible as leprosy. The two are distinctly different. The truth is that the actual words in the Hebrew and the Greek, translated leprosy in the Authorised Version, have nothing to do with what we know as modern leprosy. The original words might have indicated something identifiable and understandable to that early age, but to the western medical world of today they have no clear clinical features whereby a proper diagnosis could be made and the condition confidently identified. In the Old Testament the word is *tsara'ath* and what it means is not known, but quite evidently it refers to some disease of the skin.

The symptoms of the disease described in the Bible have no counterpart in the disease of modern leprosy. The Bible disease not only affected the skin of human beings, but also in some way contaminated and spread in wool and linen and even in the walls of buildings. Again nothing like this has ever occurred in modern leprosy. In the Bible disease the priest had the duty of inspecting the symptoms at seven day intervals in order to determine whether the condition had worsened or was so improved as to end the quarantine.

But in true leprosy the development of the symptoms, whether for the worse or the better, would never be swift enough to allow a change to be observed and a decision made thereon at an interval of seven days. True leprosy is just not like this.

Whether the word *tsara'ath* always referred to exactly the same condition is not clear. For example, in Israel it involved strict segregation; yet Naaman the Syrian, who is described as a leper,

87

seems to carry on his life with no interference. Naaman's disease fell upon Gehazi, and it was passed on to Gehazi's descendants, but Gehazi seems to have continued his service after being infected. Often, in the Bible, it is a disease associated with sin or punishment, or it is used as a sign from God. Think of Moses and Miriam. There never seems to be any human cure for this disease. If deliverance comes, it comes by an act of God. Even under the Law of Moses there is no treatment — there is separation and in due course healing may come. The priest is not a doctor, he is simply a registrar. One thing seems quite clear — it was something to be feared in ancient times. There is a sense of loathing associated with it. A kind of mystery attached to it. Who knows what it is and from whence it comes and by what means it is transmitted? Nobody really knows.

The Word in the New Testament

In the New Testament the equivalent of the Hebrew *tsara'ath* is *lepra* (you can see where the word leprosy comes from) and apparently it means scaly or scabbed. There are several references in the New Testament to people suffering from the condition, but again the information reveals nothing about the disease to enable it to be identified. It does seem clear that the symptoms of true leprosy are not discovered in what is said about the New Testament *lepra*. Why was the word *lepra* used to translate the Hebrew *tsara'ath* in the Septuagint version of the Bible written wholly in Greek? Probably because it was the best word at that time to describe a scaly condition or a scabby eruption of the skin. So they settled for *lepra*. Try to understand the difficulty of finding a word in one language to describe something in another language about which virtually nothing is known.

People who had this disease in New Testament times seem to be separated and isolated — as they were in the Old Testament arrangements. It looks as though the provisions under the Law are still being applied, at least to some extent. When the Man of Nazareth cleansed the lepers he was anxious that they should satisfy the priests of the recovered condition and secure official release from the segregation. To quote his own words in giving the instructions: "as Moses commanded." As in the Old Testament, the New Testament shows no cure for the disease, except by the power of

God. In New Testament times it was accomplished by Messiah and his apostles. The references to cures of the disease are confined exclusively to the Gospels.

One other thing — the cures, when they came, were nearly always described as a cleansing. Jesus, when sending evidence to John Baptist, says: "The lepers are cleansed." There are one or two exceptions to this rule but almost always the sick are cured but the lepers are cleansed. This certainly seems to set the disease apart as something different from all other maladies afflicting mankind. There is about it a mystery. Not only a condition of physical disability, but within it some kind of uncleanness. To be fair, it should be said that the disease which today is called leprosy — that is true leprosy, probably existed in New Testament times, but it is not the condition to which the word *lepra* was applied by the New Testament writers.

The Modern Versions

As we have seen, the Authorised Version settled for the word leprosy to describe this mysterious disease, but some modern versions of the Bible, aware no doubt of the uncertainty, have used other words such as "malignant skin disease" or "chronic skin disease" or just "skin disease", and where it refers to the contamination of material or walls then "mould" or "mildew". It has to be recognised that these descriptions do not convey the sense of the condition of uncleanness nor its awfulness, nor the element of mystery, which is without doubt part of this disease. The problem is that really there is no English word which can be commissioned to serve in the cause of an accurate definition of the disease.

To summarise — it seems clear that the disease of Bible leprosy was a physical blemish in the skin of human beings, which also in some strange way infected materials, though there is no reference to material infection in the New Testament. Furthermore, an element of ceremonial uncleanness was involved, especially in the Old Testament. The cure and the cleansing come from God, never by human skill or human power. It would be satisfying if we knew more but the Bible is silent. When all is said and done it remains a mystery.

Modern Leprosy

By way of contrast, and to emphasise the difference between the mysterious disease of the Bible and what must be called true leprosy, here are some facts about the latter condition.

It is a disease which attacks human beings almost exclusively, and affects the skin, tissues, mucous membranes and the nerves. There are two kinds — one is called tuberculoid and the other lepromatus. The first named is relatively mild, compared with the other. This mild one is bad enough but it does not have the disastrous results that follow from the other. Furthermore, tuberculoid leprosy is sometimes self healing. Lepromatus is much more severe, and instead of ever being self healing, gets progressively worse as time goes by. There is also a condition which is in between the two, where parts of both are in evidence.

The Cause and Effect

The disease affects the skin and the limbs and it causes swellings which result in growths and sometimes deformity. It can cause destruction of the nerves, blindness and ulcers. Ulcers sometimes occur in the mouth and throat, causing a complete blockage of the passage. In its very worst forms it results in loss of limbs, such as toes or feet and fingers and hands. As to the cause of the disease, the guilty bacteria was discovered in 1872 by a man named Hansen and since that time the disease has often been called Hansen's disease. The germ is very similar to the one that causes tuberculosis. Great efforts have been made to produce the bacteria in a laboratory so that a safe vaccine might actually be made. The report is that progress is slow and difficult. Of course it is always possible that by the time these sentences are in print they may be out of date. If that should prove to be the case, the writer would rejoice.

Along the pathway towards a cure for this distressing disease there are several discarded remedies, but since about the late 1930s the emphasis has been upon chemotherapy, that is the use of sulfone drugs. Quite obviously the final chapter upon the cure of this ancient and modern disease has not been written, and if the foregoing sounds very much like a medical dictionary or encyclopaedia, that judgment would be correct, for that is from where the information has been taken. It appears that the disease occurs at all ages and in both sexes. It now exists mostly in Africa, India, Central and South America and on a smaller scale in the Middle East. The last recorded case in Great Britain was in the middle of the eighteenth century.

Probably the most up-to-date attitudes upon leprosy are expressed in a memorandum from the British Department of Health and Social Security, which makes the following points:

1. Leprosy is a normally curable disease.
2. It is only slightly contagious.
3. If it is treated in time it need not result in disfiguration.
4. Only a few people need continue treatment for life.
5. As it is slow to develop it does take considerable time to treat.
6. Patients with leprosy who are undergoing treatment, can have it at home and can continue normal family life and work.

This is so different from what might be regarded as the traditional view of leprosy that the writer felt that to omit it would not help towards a balanced understanding of true leprosy. It also marks, once again, the difference between true leprosy and that disease in the Bible which is leprosy so-called.

Bible "leprosy"

For the remainder of this chapter, in order to indicate that reference is being made to the Bible condition called leprosy, the word will be in quotation marks.

In the Old Testament the method of dealing with "leprosy" is very precise, especially under the Law of Moses. This is not the place to go into all the details, but in Leviticus chapters 13 and 14 full instructions are set out.

Summing it up it amounted to this, that where there was a suspicion of "leprosy" and it was confirmed, the person was put into quarantine for seven days. If after two inspections of seven day intervals the disease seemed to be passing away, the person was set free from quarantine, after the washing of garments. On the other hand, if the condition worsened and the symptoms were stronger and the infection appeared to be spreading, the person was declared to be a "leper". That meant they had to live outside the camp of Israel in isolation. A kind of isolation hospital. In these chapters there seems to be a recognition of two particular conditions. One is called "old leprosy" and appears to be the worst kind and the other is called "white leprosy", the milder kind. In this latter case the health of the person appears to remain fairly normal and it did not demand isolation. Then, in addition, there is "leprosy" of garments. It seems that garments which were used by the sufferers became spotted and infected, if they came into direct contact with sores and wounds.

The Biblical Instructions

The isolation which the Law imposed upon those who were confirmed "lepers", shows how careful God is for the welfare of His people. They must be protected from the contamination effects of the disease. At the same time, every consideration was to be given to the person in isolation. Compassion was at the root of all the recuperative procedures. The opening verses of Leviticus 14 show the loving care with which the separated person is to be received back into the community, once the healing is confirmed. It is not just a matter of the ending of a diseased condition. The ceremony of purification is saying something important about fellowship in the brotherhood of Israel. Remember, the Israelite's attachment to the Tabernacle and the holy things of God was severed during the separation and therefore the recovery was comparable to a new lease of religious life — almost a resurrection from a living death to a newness of life.

The Spiritual Counterpart

That reference to resurrection turns the consideration towards the spiritual associations with "leprosy". All down the ages Bible commentators of varying kinds have seen "leprosy" as a symbol of sin. How far this is justified the reader must judge for himself. Recollect the Old Testament reference to garments being spotted by the disease. It has often been pointed out that in the letter of Jude, where the writer refers to sinful practices, he uses the figure "the garment spotted by the flesh". Is Jude thinking back to Leviticus and the spot of "leprosy"? Again in the Ephesian letter something similar emerges. In chapter 5 of that letter the Apostle Paul is making reference to the ultimate sinlessness of the saints, and he says "without spot and without blemish". Is this the spot of "leprosy" used as a symbol for sin in humanity? Jewish expositors of the Old Testament say, "Every sin is leprosy, a spot upon the soul".

Then something else — the regular use in the New Testament of the word *cleanse* to describe "leprosy" being cured or "lepers" being healed, as though it was not just a disease, but in some way a defilement. Alongside this has to be put the word of the Apostle John about pardon for sin and the processs of renewal. He says, "If we confess our sins, he is faithful and just to forgive us our sins, and to *cleanse* us from all unrighteousness".

Expositors have fixed upon these references and have seen in them some certainty that "leprosy" has a spiritual counterpart in sin. Going on from this they analyse the correspondence between the two forces by stressing these similarities — the element of mystery; the manifestation and the effect and the attitude of the Law. The case is argued like this:

"Leprosy" and Sin

In the Bible "leprosy" is a mystery. It exists but it is not explained. Suddenly it is there and just as suddenly it isolates men from their fellows. How it comes, and why here and not there, no one knows. Why some are affected and others escape, who can tell? At first sight this correspondence with sin — the mystery — does not seem to be well proven, since the origin of sin is well known and its effect is part of every person's experience. Indeed, some might even be inclined to say that sin is the one thing we know all about only too well.

But to be fair, that is not really the case. It is undeniable that we know how sin started and how it came into the world. We are able to notice one man's misadventure in Genesis chapter 3. We know what Adam and Eve did to become sinful. What is not so clear is what made Cain sinful — or for that matter Adam's other children? Sin is everywhere in everybody by one single act of disobedience. According to Acts 17 there is a sense in which men are the offspring of God, and yet in the very fibre of their being they are sin stricken. And stricken is the right word. Sin atrophies human powers; paralyses human endeavour; poisons human aspirations and prevents the realisation of the best human ambitions.

The malady is centred in the human will, in the heart and in the mind. Jesus said, "Wherefore think ye evil in your hearts?" as a rebuke to the Scribes. Again he said: "For out of the heart proceed evil thoughts, murders, adulteries, fornications, thefts, false witness, blasphemies."

In announcing the right treatment for this central malady, Paul says, "Be ye transformed by the *renewing of your mind*". When the eye sins it starts in the mind. When the hand steals it starts in the heart. Jesus told it plainly. Furthermore he said this: that the sin of adultery is not firstly a sin of the flesh, sensual and physical. It is that; but first it is a sin of the spirit, conceived and committed in the heart. Somehow sin is inherited and passes from one generation to another. Since it is so much a matter of mind and will, no one could be blamed for asking how it is transmitted. This child, say one week old, will be a sinner because of one act of disobedience perpetrated a long time ago when the world was very young. There is a strangeness about it, this malady with a thousand manifestations. Let us be honest — we do not know all about it by any means.

The Manifestations

The reference to the child should remind us how early the symptoms appear. The petty jealousies, the white lies, the childish tantrums are all foretastes of forces which later on may curse and dominate the child's will. There is an old saying that the child is father to the man, and this is often true at the level of weakness and wilfulness.

Faculties misused in the early years may become lawlessness unrestrained in later adult life. When family discipline is left behind, slowly the submerged forces of rebellion become open and wilful. Say what you will, there is a strangeness about it which we cannot really fathom.

No wonder John calls it "the mystery of lawlessness". About sin and about "leprosy" there is a mystery, and about the manifestation there is a correspondence which it is difficult to deny. No doubt that is why the old expositors saw the disease as a symbol of sin.

The Effect under the Law

From the Biblical records it is plain that one of the effects of "leprosy" was to exclude those who suffered from it from fellowship with their fellow men. They were isolated and cut off from association with others. Something similar is true of sin. Who does not know that in the more devilish and sensual manifestations it has the effect of outlawing fellowship and friendship, most noticeably on the part of the sinner. He is self isolated, withdrawn, a man apart by his own will. In the Bible when sin is being discussed we find words like "hardened", or "past feeling", or "consciences seared with a hot iron". All this draws attention to the soul indifferent to sympathy and compassion. A barrier, sin-built, between the failing one and his sympathising brethren. Sometimes sinners become benumbed and every good influence is checked by an armour of hardness and despair. Even the loving discipline of the ecclesia is of no avail. Could the isolation of "leprosy" typify the separation of sin?

Remember that under the Law of Moses, when the "leper" was isolated, he was separated not only from men, but in a sense from God, insofar that he was cut off from the outward and organised worship of God in the community. This may very well reinforce the correspondence with sin. Fellowship with God is harmed by sin if it remains unpardoned and especially if it is justified by guile. And sometimes in the hardening process, guile is used as a defence. Think what it does. To the sinner, in the consciousness of what he has done and the excuses he is making, God seems remote. The vision is clouded, the insight is dim. Sometimes the fact and force of God seems far away. The distance is measured in light years. An iron curtain has been erected by the fact of the transgression. In the very worst cases, to the fevered mind the situation seems irretrievable. Perhaps it was something like this that fixed Judas in his awful destiny. The place of meeting seems barred by the enormity of the divide. The pathway back to concord and joy is rejected by the very one who needs it most. Unclean, blemished, isolated — such the "leper" may feel, and such is the sinner without God.

So all down the ages men have felt that in these ways "leprosy" reveals the nature of sin.

The Double Cure

In the New Testament, one thing about sin is abundantly clear. It cannot be cured by men. Men can deal with sins but they cannot deal with Sin. They can comfort the sinners but they cannot deal with the infirmity. Medical science can treat the symptoms but it cannot remove the disease. People can sign an undertaking to shed weight and sometimes succeed, but giving a pledge to eliminate sin is doomed to failure. Most sensible people have a clear conviction that here is something beyond the power of men to conquer. They are prepared to live with it and hope for the best. They call it human nature and admit that at its worst it is a blight on the world, a virus deep in the system. The Bible is categoric — by it people are destroyed and so are nations.

Come back to the process of cleansing under the Hebrew Law. As we have already indicated, it is made clear in Leviticus chapter 14. The priest went out of the camp to the place where the "leper" was isolated, in order to inspect the sufferer's condition and, if favourable, to certify and declare that a cure had occurred. It is important to notice that the priest did not cleanse the "leper" because he could not do that. The best he could do was to inspect and certify.

If cleansing had occurred then a ceremony followed which was designed to symbolise and celebrate the "leper's" recovery and cleansing. It was clear that as no man had cleansed the "leper" it was the work of God, and the "leper" was to recognise it in the sacrifices offered. In Leviticus 14 the instructions are precise. Two birds are to be provided for sacrifice — one to be offered, the other to be set free.

Then the cedarwood, which is impervious to decay, and therefore the symbol of incorruption and strength. The meaning of the scarlet is regarded by some expositors as representing life, health and beauty. Others have different ideas.

About the hyssop there is more certainty. It was a plant of healing and fragrance and perhaps represented the final cure from God. Indeed we sing about it in this very way: "Do thou with hyssop sprinkle me, I shall be cleansed so". It is an allusion to Psalm 51. So by these things in the brotherhood of Israel, the cleansing effected by God was celebrated under the old law.

The Shadow and the Substance

There are disparities between the shadow and the substance, which have the effect of heightening the truth more surely. The High Priest of the Universe does not go without the camp to inspect and certify the "leper" cleansed. He goes without the camp to *cleanse the "leper" altogether*.

This is not the place to enter a description of the doctrine of the Atonement. The truth is that the High Priest, the Man of Nazareth, came to the place of isolation; the place where the "leper" is alone and cast off; the place of shame and disgrace, to cleanse and save and recover. It has been told hundreds of times in better words than these. If the broken man will cry "Lord thou canst make me clean", the Lord will do it. To quote a remembered sentence from long ago: "By some mystery of his own life and death, he takes the agony himself and purifies it, cancels it and ends it".

Thousands of cleansed people will testify that this is true. The spirit that once was restless and lawless utters the word of submission, and through the blessed touch of the redeemer, is cleansed, renewed, and remade, and comes at last into the City of God, the brotherhood of the Saints and into the blessed joy of the Kingdom of God.

25

HOW TO AVOID DISEASE AND

KEEP HEALTHY

THIS is where the body and the soul are at their closest, because what is essentially true about one is essentially true about the other. As the Foreword said — Man is one whole. Natural life needs certain elemental forces to sustain it and keep it robust; and the same is true of the spiritual life. What makes it so interesting is that in the Bible the words which are used to describe the one are also used to describe the other. As this chapter proceeds, this principle will become evident.

The Right Food

It goes without saying that the condition of the body is regulated by the quality of the food taken to sustain it. Nowadays considerable emphasis is laid upon the need to avoid foods which in the long run are detrimental to good health and which encourage diseases such as heart attacks, strokes, occlusion of the arteries, hypertension etc. The things which our grandparents held to be good nourishing food are now reckoned to be highly dangerous. The writer remembers that as a boy he was urged to fill himself with animal fat as a defence against "consumption". Such a course today would be counted madness. Notwithstanding, he has to confess some disappointment that a number of his favourite menus, enjoyed for half a century, are now on the banned list.

Never before has it been proclaimed so forcibly that what we eat makes us what we are. So it is with the soul, the spiritual part of man. It is nourished by that which comes to it from outside and it needs to be the right kind of nourishment. The word of Christ Jesus is paramount: he said, "Man shall not live by bread alone, but by every word that proceedeth out of the mouth of God doth man live".

This is the staff of spiritual life, quoted from the book of Deuteronomy. The Apostle Peter says as new born babes we are to desire the sincere milk of the word that we may grow thereby (1 Peter 2:2). In the Word of God is sustenance for every level of life and every stage of development.

Paul wrote to young Timothy that if he followed the practice of faithful living he would be "nourished up in the words of faith and sound doctrine " (1 Timothy 4:6). Timothy was a young man at this time but the words are true of all — young and old, leaders and led, strong and weak. Jesus said, "I am the bread of life". He said he was the disciple's manna. His teaching, his example, his priesthood — that means the living word and the written word — these are the forces which give nourishment to the new man. To the Colossians Paul wrote: "Let the word of Christ dwell in you richly in all wisdom" (3:16). So the simple diet of the Word of God, taken with enjoyment every day; the meat and drink of the spirit, will, according to the New Testament writers, enable the disciple to keep healthy and grow. It means that dusty Bibles and neglected Bible Classes and lack of time to give to feeding on the Word of life, is the recipe for sickness.

The Right Atmosphere

We take fresh air for granted, but when it is in short supply the result is serious. Think of big cities before the Clean Air Act was enacted. People in London died in their thousands from bronchitis and related diseases, because of bad air, smoke laden and polluted. Recollect this — in old films where London is represented at night, it is always shown as full of fog. Those days are virtually gone — the 'pea-souper' is a bad memory. As a result thousands of lives have been saved. Then again, when the sick are recuperating they are sent to the seaside or the country, because the air is fresh and pure. There is a phrase in the Bible, "the breath of life", and it is utterly fundamental to good health. Breathing air keeps us alive and breathing good air keeps us more alive and well. That it why smoking is such a handicap to good health. The lungs are filled with elements which irritate and harm. Those who give up the habit are almost always soon telling of better health and the discovery of how good their food tastes, especially the new flavour of this or that. Those who cannot give up the habit deserve our sympathy and help. Perhaps this is the most telling illustration that breathing polluted air results in impaired health and proves how vital it is that if we intend to keep breathing we should breathe the best air available.

So it is with the soul. Spiritual health thrives in the right atmosphere. Things which pollute also choke the spirit.

Where the breathing space is full of worldliness, the possibilities of glowing health are retarded. The right atmosphere does not mean a bed of roses with never a setback and where everything is ideal. Character is formed by overcoming the circumstances which are adverse and by mastering the things which are antagonistic and sometimes hostile. The hot-house atmosphere is likely to produce a spiritual life, tender and sappy, which in times of testing soon droops and withers. Usually the atmosphere is good where the saints are together in fellowship. There the spirit is renewed and stimulated. There the air is free from worldly pollution. There the redeemed breathe in the elements which are related to the Kingdom of God. There the air is love infected and refreshed by faith. There the windows are open and there is commerce with heaven. There the weak hands are lifted up and the feeble knees are strengthened. This is the atmosphere which purifies the circulation and keeps the spiritual mind clear. Remember this, that the conflict in the life of faith is between the urge to please self and the call to please God. One thing that helps the disciple in his ability to please God is the mutual encouragement of his comrades in the faith.

Sharing a common belief, having one hope, impulsed by love gives strength to the resolution. Pondering the pearl of great price, together. Comparing experiences in the good fight of faith. Confessing faults one to another. Deliberating on how to put the grand theory into practice in a busy and corrupting world. Praying together in worship, thanksgiving and petition. All this is the atmosphere that fills the soul with spiritual oxygen and keeps the pulse steady. To the Corinthians Paul said, "Cleanse yourselves from all filthiness of the flesh and spirit" (2 Corinthians 7:1). He was not speaking particularly of a filthy atmosphere but because atmospheres do get filthy, it must be included. What it means today is this: 'Get your spiritual air conditioning in good working order'. James said, ''Pure religion and undefiled before God and the Father is this, to visit the fatherless and widows in their affliction, and to keep himself unspotted from the world'' (1:27). Pure religion thrives best where the good wind of God blows through the crooks and crannies of our striving discipleship and keeps the air clean and fresh. Fit to inhale to make us healthy.

The Right Exercise

To jog or not to jog, that is the question — for some! But apart from the wisdom of jogging, the value of exercise as a support of good health can hardly be denied. It is good to eat rightly and breathe rightly, but if there is no exercise, the muscles get flabby, the sinews get sluggish, the joints tend to seize up, especially in the over-forties. Most of all, exercise stimulates the pulse rates and keeps the heart muscles in trim.

Exercise makes the body supple, and it also helps in preventing excess fat becoming a burden. By exercise weight is shed, the system is strengthened, the constitution is toned up. The benefit is based on a simple principle — some things get better with use. Stagnation leads to impotence. Powers not used tend to atrophy. Think of the man in the synagogue with the withered arm. Jesus said, ''Stretch forth thy hand'' and ended the poor man's disability. Supposing the healed man, delighted with his new found ability, but worried lest he should wear it out by use, wrapped it up and put it in a sling to preserve it. We know that in a few months it would be as useless as before, withered and wasted through lack of exercise. It speaks for itself — people who could exercise and do not, are doing themselves a mischief and it will show, sooner or later.

Godly Exercise

In 1 Timothy 4:8 Paul says, ''Bodily exercise profiteth little''. That does not contradict the foregoing nor is Paul wanting to disparage bodily exercise. When he says little he means *little by comparison with the exercise of the spirit.*

Actually, in other versions it sounds better than the Authorised Version. ''Physical training, indeed, is of some benefit'' (C. B.

Williams). "Bodily fitness has a certain value" (J. B. Phillips).

This letter was written to Timothy when he had oversight of the ecclesia at Ephesus and there one of the foremost activities was the development of the human body to make it fit and beautiful. This was the Greek ideal. Remember it was in Greece that the Olympic Games originated. So in a place strongly given over to bodily exercise Paul says to Timothy, "Exercise *thyself* unto godliness". Godliness is God-*like*-ness and Paul is exhorting Timothy so to act and move in the ecclesia at Ephesus that his life approximates to the character of God. This is based on a great Bible principle, namely, that men become like the God they worship and obey, good or bad. It is made clear in Psalm 115. After describing the insensate idols of the heathen nations and their utter impotence, the psalmist says, "They that make them shall be like unto them" (verse 8, R.V.). The other side of the principle is seen in 1 John 3:2 in words full of inspired hope: "We shall be like him".

Whichever way it is, men become like the God they worship. That is why the right spiritual exercise leads men to Godlikeness. Things which have a common purpose take on a common likeness. Think what spiritual exercise means. It means making sure that such abilities as you have are used to advance the cause of Christ and never to hinder it. Working and not slacking in his business in the world. In working life and career business, executing every transaction in a Godly fashion on true principles. In prosperity not being greedy; in poverty not being soured. Laying the measurement of God upon all the false values of a society dominated by materialism. Having time for the work of the Truth — redeeming it because the days are evil. Busy for the gospel and glad to get tired in its service. This is exercise indeed.

Of course there are other passages in the New Testament which stress the importance of spiritual exercise.

> *"Know ye not that they which run in a race run all, but one receiveth the prize? So run, that ye may obtain. And every man that striveth for the mastery is temperate in all things. Now they do it to obtain a corruptible crown; but we an incorruptible. I therefore so run, not as uncertainly; so fight I, not as one that beateth the air: but I keep under my body, and bring it into subjection: lest that by any means, when I have preached to others, I*

myself should be a castaway.''   (1 Corinthians 9:24 – 27)

Nowadays, with the opportunity to see the world's finest athletes from our armchairs, it must be evident how strong is the competition and how dedicated the contenders have to be to succeed. Training involves ceaseless practice, careful living and strict abstinence from the things which impair fitness. Paul says to the spiritual athelete, "So run that ye may obtain". Which means, put everything you have into gaining the victory. In verse 26 there is an allusion to boxing: "So fight I, not as one that beateth the air". In a modern version this reads: "I fight to win, I am not just shadow boxing or playing around". It stresses once again that spiritual exercise is serious, persistent, and determined. Furthermore, it emphasises that there is a kind of exercise which rightly named *is* playing around.

"Wherefore seeing we also are compassed about with so great a cloud of witnesses, let us lay aside every weight, and the sin which doth so easily beset us, and let us run with patience the race that is set before us, looking unto Jesus the author and finisher of our faith. ''   (Hebrews 12:1,2)

Weights are things which hold the athlete back, which hinder or slow down. Things which ought to be shed in the cause of victory. They may not be wrong in themselves but in the race they are a serious drawback. For example there is nothing wrong with hobnail boots or an overcoat, but the athlete who wore them to race in would be reckoned more to have head disease than foot trouble. "Weights" sometimes means flirting with temptation; toying with dangerous things. The Hebrew man says, "Strip it away".

"Ye were running well; who did hinder you that ye should not obey the truth?''   (Galatians 5:7, R.V.)

One modern version puts it, "Ye were running the race well; who has cast a stumbling block in your way? who has turned you aside from your obedience to the truth?"

What had turned them aside was the bad advice of some of their trainers. The coaching was based on wrong principles. They had been enticed into a system which by its very nature denied the forces which make for victory. They were returning to a set of rules which were sure to bring unfitness and failure. Learning from the Galatians should teach the athlete to get the right manual, follow it faithfully and keep to the example of the tested leader.

The word which is translated 'exercise' in the first letter to Timothy is the Greek word *gymnasia*. A man who seeks to be a real gymnast must be a dedicated man. A man who is spasmodic, half hearted, neglectful, or casual, gymnastically is likely to fail. So underlying the ideas of spiritual exercise are devotion, endurance, discipline, self-control, purity.

In the end, when all is said and done, proficiency does not come from speculating but from doing. Following the rules in the mind does not do much for the spiritual muscles. It demands *active* fidelity to the principles of spiritual health. It is faith manifested in sustained doing of the word.

Things to Remember

One of the blessed benefits of health is growth. Bad health often brings arrested development, especially in the young. When the Apostle Peter urges disciples to ''grow in grace'' he presupposes two things — life and health. So the thing is to keep healthy because health means growth. About the objective of growth there should be no doubt. Growth is growth into the likeness of Christ Jesus. Ephesians 4 proves it: ''Speaking the truth is love ye may grow up into him in all things, which is the head, even Christ'' (verse 15). It means that given that the forces of life and health are truly at work, then the soul of man, the new man, will bit by bit be growing into the likeness of the Son of God. In the course of natural health people from time to time have a check-up.

Here is the spiritual check-up: ''Am I more like Jesus Christ than I was?'' This is the question that ought to be asked on a regular basis. Not in the market place but in the closet. Honestly with yourself alone. Of course you can take the opinion of true friends — that is, those who will tell you the truth, which is a sign of true friendship. But in the end the diagnosis is best reached with an audience of one.

These are the test questions. Am I easier to live with? Am I more compassionate? Am I more generous? Am I angry about those things which offend the purity of God? Do I feel more the burden of those who are lost? Am I really thrilled by the prospect of the imminent coming of the Messiah? Is the kingdom of God truly the master passion of my life? Is my loyalty to all the things of Truth stronger than it was or weaker? Who are the people with whom I have the closest relationship? Honest answers to these questions could tell the disciple how well he is growing, say in comparison with three years back. Remember, being static is not really the objective. The objective is growth. And it should be a divinely natural thing if there is life and health.

Think of Paul in Philippians:

> *"Not as though I had already attained, either were already perfect . . . but this one thing I do, forgetting those things which are behind . . . I press toward the mark for the prize of the high calling of God in Christ Jesus."*
>
> (3:12-14)

Paul recognises he is still making progress and he needs to press on, forgetting the past, looking onward to the future. Remember that in the final analysis everything is being sought and achieved for love's sake; the constraint of that love which was given fully without reserve by the Great Physician. By his stripes we have been healed. Spiritual health has been made possible by that life which was won out of death by the Redeemer who bore our sicknesses. This health is good indeed.

So to all the readers of this little book the writer has one wish — Good Health.